The Music of
Emily Dickinson's
Poems and Letters

The Music of Emily Dickinson's Poems and Letters

A Study of Imagery and Form

by CAROLYN LINDLEY COOLEY

McFarland & Company, Inc., Publishers
Jefferson, North Carolina, and London

Library of Congress Cataloguing-in-Publication Data

Cooley, Carolyn Lindley, 1933–
    The music of Emily Dickinson's poems and letters :
a study of imagery and form / by Carolyn Lindley Cooley.
      p. cm.
    Includes bibliographical references (p.) and index.

    ISBN 0-7864-1491-X (softcover : 50# alkaline paper)

    1. Dickinson, Emily, 1830–1886—Knowledge—Music.
2. Dickinson, Emily, 1830–1886—Musical settings.   3. Music
and literature—History—19th century.   4. Music in literature.
I. Title.
PS1541.Z5C67 2003
811'.4—dc21

                         2002155758

British Library cataloguing data are available

Cover art: (foreground) ©2003 Art Today, (background) ©2003 Artville.

Manufactured in the United States of America

McFarland & Company, Inc., Publishers
  Box 611, Jefferson, North Carolina 28640
   www.mcfarlandpub.com

To Rob,
who adds music to my life every day

Acknowledgments

My genuine gratitude goes to three Dickinson scholars who have taken interest in my book and have encouraged me along the way. Of these scholars, David Porter was the first to read my manuscript and to urge publication. His sincere enthusiasm for my project, and his advice and availability, have made him the best of all mentors.

One of my life's great pleasures was spending two hours with Richard Sewall in his home in Bethany, Connecticut, where we discussed all things Dickinson. His tender, interpretive reading of "I cannot live with You —" still rings in my ears. He and I had tears in our eyes when he finished, the best of tributes to the poet we both love. Because Sewall's biography of Emily Dickinson is such a vital tool for any Dickinson research, I particularly appreciated his assurance that my research was innovative and worthwhile, for he told me, "If I had to write a book on Emily Dickinson and music, I wouldn't even know where to start."

I am grateful to Willis J. Buckingham for reading my manuscript and for making constructive comments on Chapter III, which is based on his documentary study of nineteenth-century reviews of Dickinson's poems and letters. His observation that my work "sharply brings into awareness how important music is in Dickinson's poetry and in responses to it (and especially in 1890s responses)" was very meaningful to me, as was his added remark, "I (and I think many others) had simply overlooked it as part of an outmoded, impressionistic vocabulary about poetry." These three scholars have made enormous contributions to the field of Dickinson studies, and their support of my endeavor is especially significant to me.

I am indebted to the many composers who shared with me the compositional techniques they adopted in their settings to interpret Dickinson's poems in music. Their views add an important dimension to this analysis of Dickinson and music, providing an opportunity to unite the two art forms of poetry and music to create a new medium of expression. The correspondence from each composer and arranger has been deeply appreciated.

Special recognition, however, should go to the families of two of the best-known composers of Dickinson settings. Ellen Bacon, widow of Ernst Bacon, provided me with a wealth of resources which detail her husband's passion for Emily Dickinson's genius, a passion which is reflected in his numerous musical settings of her poems. These materials would have been totally unavailable to me without her generosity. The other composer to receive expanded treatment is Arthur Farwell, and two of his children have been most generous in sharing unpublished information about their father's compositional output under "Dickinson's spell." Brice Farwell sent valuable material documenting his father's almost mystical relationship to Dickinson, and Sara Farwell wrote a five-page letter expressing her recollections of the affinity her father had with Emily Dickinson and of his ardent dedication to setting her poetry to music. The insights contributed by these family members, as well as those of all of the composers, add vitality to an understanding of the close relationship existing between music and poetry.

My friends have been a very special part of this enterprise, and their interest and support have contributed more than they realize to the process which has culminated in this book. The following academic friends at the University of South Florida have graciously shared their expertise and their time with me and have always encouraged my endeavors: Jack Moore, Sara Deats, Maryhelen Harmon, Robert Figg, Ruth Banes, and Flora Zbar. Special thanks goes to Sue McCord, who always has the proper word of encouragement at the appropriate time. To Mary Alice Wise goes my deepest gratitude for instinctively knowing the right thing to do and then doing it, regardless of the cost, time, or effort. And deep appreciation is due to Elizabeth McAbee for her expertise in preparing the final manuscript for publication and for her friendship during this process.

I am indebted to Jennie Rathbun for her prompt and courteous assistance with information and materials I have needed from the Emily Dickinson Collection at the Houghton Library. I also thank Roger Stoddard, Curator of Rare Books at the Houghton, and Peter Accardo, acquisitions bibliographer there, for permission to reprint the sheets of music from Emily Dickinson's Portfolio of Music. Melissa Chivington's extensive musical knowledge provided important confirmation of my analysis of Dickinson's musical ability, which was a meaningful collaboration.

Warmest gratitude goes to my family—Laurie, Jack, Brett, Jeanne and Craig—for understanding my need to retreat from the world for a time to write this book. I especially want to express my heartfelt thankfulness to my husband Rob, for without his belief in my project and his support in every conceivable way throughout my research and writing, this book could never have been written. And finally, in their memory, I am much obliged to my parents Horace and Ruth Lindley, who offered me golden opportunities, with love.

Contents

Poetry is music written for the human voice.
—*Maya Angelou*

Preface

My early attraction to Emily Dickinson's poetry centered on the numerous ways in which her poems struck a common chord in my mind and in my heart. However, as I delved deeper into her poems and then her letters, I uncovered a magnetic connection with Dickinson which has increased my enjoyment of her work and has enlarged my vision of her multifaceted talent. To my great delight, I discovered the music of Emily Dickinson's poems and letters. Not only did I begin to respond to the rhythm of her verses, but my background in music and my affinity for poetry combined to provide a natural response to the musical imagery which is prevalent in Dickinson's prose and poetry.

Examining Dickinson's works for musical terms and imagery became a treasure hunt for me, and the rewards of that search have been indeed fulfilling. My investigation has revealed that music is a vital element in Dickinson's prose and poetry and underscores that the creative power she achieves through her application of musical terminology is undeniable. Recognizing the importance of music to Dickinson's verse can intensify a reader's awareness of the aesthetic richness of the Dickinson canon and can also provide important insights into the inherent meaning of many of her major works, while adding dimension to numerous minor ones.

Surprisingly, in view of the important role music plays in Dickinson's works, its function as a literary technique has not yet been fully explored, and what is available on this subject in biographical and critical studies is scarce and scattered. No one work has yet collated the musical influences in Dickinson's background which are later revealed within the context of her poems and letters. Yet, Dickinson herself believed that a true poet should possess the ability to "stun" oneself "With Bolts of Melody," and her penchant for this skill is one of the distinguishing hallmarks of her literary work. Through the synthesis of poetry and music, Dickinson establishes an effective method for creating her verse and an affective mode for expressing the emotional connotation of her words.

Because of the dearth of previous studies pertaining to Emily Dickinson and music, I have relied, for the most part, on primary sources for my material, particularly *The Complete Poems of Emily Dickinson*[1] and *The Letters of Emily Dickinson*,[2] both edited by Thomas H. Johnson. (The Johnson edition of the poems was chosen over the more recent R. W. Franklin edition because all of the composers in Chapter VI selected poems from the Johnson edition for their musical settings. To combine two different editions of the poems would have been, quite simply, too confusing.) In addition, Jay Leyda's two-volume work, *The Years and Hours of Emily Dickinson*, has provided me with valuable biographical material and documents relating to Dickinson and to her times. Two bibliographies, *Emily Dickinson: The Critical Revolution* by Klaus Lubbers and *Emily Dickinson's Reception in the 1890s: A Documentary History* edited by Willis J. Buckingham, have also supplied invaluable data on the growth of Dickinson's literary reputation and on the early criticism surrounding it. Although none of these works has specifically dealt with Emily Dickinson and music, I have gained some important insights on the impact of this combination by searching their pages.

There are some tangential sources which do not mention Dickinson's name at all but which serve very important functions in verifying the authentic quality of music in her verse. One of these is *Musical Influences on American Poetry* by Charmenz Lenhart, the first, and to date the only, extended study to bring together evidences of nineteenth-century American poets and their awareness of music. This work is directly concerned with those lyrical poets in America who were recognized literary figures and with their poems or that segment of their verse which reveals the influence of music. Though Lenhart does not include Dickinson in this study, her work provides the opportunity to compare the musical qualities of Dickinson's verse with musical qualities present in the works of such poets as Edgar Allan Poe, Walt Whitman, and Ralph Waldo Emerson, and these comparisons are enlightening.

Another book which might seem at first to be totally unrelated is John Hollander's study *The Untuning of the Sky: Ideas of Music in English Poetry 1500–1700*. Yet Hollander's intent to follow the development of music's role in English poetry, both as subject matter and as image, offers some insights about poetry and music in general which are applicable to music in Dickinson's poetry in particular. For instance, Hollander discusses the concept of "the music of the spheres" as being made up of consonant intervals which have the clearest and best "scale" with respect to their fundamental pitch. Dickinson apparently understood this concept, as she reveals in this letter to Susan Gilbert in 1853: "Dear Susie — I send you a little air — The 'Music of the Spheres.' They are represented above as passing thro' the sky" (L 134). Dickinson included in this letter a sketch she had made of ascending musical notations (scales) and puffs of ascending clouds.

Hollander also develops the sixteenth- and seventeenth-century idea that a metonymic use of the lute (for the lyre) to represent poetry as well as music was then, and remains, a familiar concept. This aids in the interpretation of Dickinson's Poem 261: "Put up my lute! / What of — my Music! / Since the sole ear I cared to charm — / Passive — as Granite — laps My Music — / Sobbing — will suit — as well as psalm!" Of importance also is Hollander's discussion of modality, which concerns the ability of certain musical configurations to elicit particular active or emotive responses in their hearers. In this regard, Hollander follows the gradual development of the terms "mode" (major and minor keys) and "mood" (feeling) as they unite to express the aesthetic notion that the feeling evoked by a musical or poetic work resides in the work itself. These are important concepts for an understanding of Dickinson's musical imagery in Chapter II and for comprehending the musical moods elicited by both Dickinson and the composers in Chapter VI.

Leonard Meyer amplifies this theory of the affective power of major and minor modes in his study *Emotion and Meaning in Music*. Here, Meyer confirms that from Plato down to the most recent discussions of aesthetics and the meaning of music, the majority of philosophers and critics have affirmed their belief in the ability of music to evoke emotional responses in listeners. We know that Dickinson responded emotionally to music, for she wrote, "The fascinating chill that music leaves / Is Earth's corroboration / Of Ecstasy's impediment —" (P 1480). Meyer also elaborates on the notion that the minor mode is not only associated with intense feeling in general but with the depiction of sadness, suffering, and anguish in particular, while the major mode reflects states of calm contentment and gentle joy which are considered to be the more normal human emotional states. Dickinson indicates that she understands this concept in a letter to her friend Mrs. J. G. Holland when she writes, "In adequate Music there is a Major and a Minor —" (L 370). Finally, Meyer's assertion that one can hardly fail to become aware of the striking similarity of some aspects of musical experience to other types of aesthetic experience, particularly those induced by literature, is remarkably true in Dickinson's works, for her poems and her letters reflect the intense feelings—the major and minor modes of which Meyer speaks—perhaps as well as any other American poet.

Two final studies, both by ornithologists, add authenticity to Dickinson's musical acuity. First in consideration is Poul Bondesen's *North American Bird Songs*. Though Bondesen is not concerned with Dickinson or with poetry at all, his findings verify what Dickinson expresses so beautifully in her numerous poems about bird song. In his introduction, Bondeson says, "The bird song is a kind of music—it may be enjoyed directly with a thought of pattern rhythm and character of sounds, just as is the case with the music performed by man." He later affirms that "a bird's song is a true song of full biological and communicational value,"[3] which is a concept Dickinson understood and expressed when she wrote, "The Bird her punctual music brings / And lays it in its place — / Its place is in the Human Heart / And in the Heavenly Grace —" (P 1585) and "I have a Bird in spring / Which for myself doth sing —" (P 5). Dickinson's many poems and letters that concern bird song confirm what the animal psychologist

4

Wallace Craig wrote, that "bird song is undoubtedly music, but it is not merely 'tone-music,' but also 'poetic music' in which the accent is on construction: pattern and rhythm, tempo and tone character...."[4]

Ornithologist W. H. Thorpe sought to answer the question, "Is there anything behind this universal popular conviction that birds sing, in the sense of making music?" in his book *Bird-Song: The Biology of Vocal Communication and Expression in Birds*. Though his study is far-removed from Dickinson and her poetry, he offers some important insights which clarify Dickinson's knowledge of bird song and her application of that knowledge in her poetry and in her letters. For example, Thorpe presents evidence of a very fundamental characteristic of auditory communication that applies equally to both birds and humans—namely that "fairly shrill sounds which rise in pitch and have a fairly restricted lower and higher frequency ... strike us as encouraging, reassuring or cheerful; and sounds which descend over a considerable frequency strike us as mournful, sad or pathetic."[5] Bird song, then, expresses major and minor musical moods in a way similar to human song. Dickinson certainly recognized this quality of bird song, and she wrote about it in poem after poem and in letter after letter. For example, in "The Morning after Woe —" Dickinson observes, "The Birds declaim their Tunes — / Pronouncing every word / Like Hammers — Did they know they fell / Like Litanies of Lead —" (P 364). The minor mood of this poem is replaced by the major mood of Poem 1265: "The most triumphant Bird I ever knew or met / Embarked upon a twig today / And till Dominion set / I famish to behold so eminent a sight / And sang for nothing scrutable / But intimate Delight." Countless examples could be adduced to illustrate that Dickinson not only understood the moods of the bird songs she heard, but that she accurately interpreted them in her poetry as well.

One final example from Thorpe's study confirms Dickinson's knowledge and perception of bird song as music and offers an opportunity to verify more fully the meaning behind one of Dickinson's enigmatic poems. Thorpe asserts, "The judgment of musical beauty is a personal judgment depending upon an emotional relationship between the music and the hearer, derived from his past experience and social environment, which largely determines his decision as to what is beautiful."[6] Dickinson says the same thing in this poetic way: "To hear an Oriole sing / May be a common thing — / Or only a divine.... The Fashion of the Ear / Attireth that it hear / in Dun, or fair — / ... So whether it be Rune, / Or whether it be none / Is of within..." (P 526). That Dickinson comprehended the intricacies of bird song, in both a technical and an aesthetic way, adds an important dimension to the authenticity and to the meaning of her many poems concerning the music of the birds.

These sources have enriched and added depth to my work, which focuses on the musical imagery, musical quality, musical form, and musical meter inherent in Dickinson's verse, all of which, in turn, have inspired composers to create musical settings for her poems. Carlton Lowenberg's reference book *Musicians Wrestle Everywhere* provided valuable resource material leading me into correspondence with a selected group of composers about their individual musical settings of Dickinson's poetry, material which forms the basis of Chapter VI.

All of these elements confirm the fact that Emily Dickinson deserves to take her rightful place with the other major musical poets of the nineteenth century. In a substantial way, the insights which these findings illuminate about Dickinson's relationships with music verify Richard Sewall's statement that Emily Dickinson "appears in ever-widening perspective, and her stature grows. She comes to us increasingly as the summation of a culture, not (as she was long regarded) a minor and freakish offshoot."[7]

CHAPTER I

Musical Background
of Dickinson's Life and Times

By infusing her prose and poetry with musical imagery, terms, and techniques, Dickinson becomes aligned with some of the most important and recognized writers of her day, for many of the major nineteenth-century American poets gave some evidence of musical influence, directly or indirectly, on their verse. During the nineteenth century, music was widely recognized as having a profound affinity with poetry. While eighteenth-century critics had turned to painting in order to specify the character of poetry, nineteenth-century thinkers established poetry as the music of the soul. Characteristic of the century was an interest in music by poets, and an equally intense interest in poetry by musicians, establishing a creative duality unknown since the Renaissance. That Dickinson qualifies as a participant in this revival can be seen by some brief comments on the musical tendencies of four major nineteenth-century poets who may, or may not, have influenced the musicality of her own works.

Among nineteenth-century poets, none spoke more strongly of the assistance music offered verse than Edgar Allan Poe. In "The Poetic Principle," Poe wrote of "the certainty that Music, in its various modes of metre, rhythm, and rhyme, is of so vast a moment in Poetry as never to be wisely rejected." He also believed that "the union of Poetry with Music in the popular sense" provides "the widest field for the Poetic development." Dickinson, an avid reader of numerous newspapers and periodicals of her day, must have read some of Poe's poems when they were printed in *The Springfield Republican*. However, Dickinson wrote to her literary friend Thomas Wentworth Higginson in 1879, "Of Poe, I know too little to think" (L 622), her only known comment on the poet, thereby dismissing him as a possible influence on the musical quality of her own poetry.

Another potential influence on the musical quality of Dickinson's verse would be Walt Whitman, for to music Whitman owes "his diffuseness, his line, his form for verse, the inspiration for many of his poems, his rhythms, and some of the impassioned quality of his verse."[1] This description would as well suit Dickinson's debt to music. However, in replying to a letter from Higginson in which he inquired if she had read this "new, audacious poet," Dickinson wrote in April of 1862, "You speak of Mr. Whitman — I never read his Book — but was told that he was disgraceful" (L 261). Though Whitman's and Dickinson's names are often associated together in contemporary literary commentaries, the common bond of music so prominent in both of their works has not yet been firmly established.

Ralph Waldo Emerson, like Dickinson, employed musical symbols and metaphors to express the elation he experienced in the world of nature. He also made numerous references to music in his verses, his essays, and his private journals, and some of these would have been accessible to Emily Dickinson, for the family library contained four major works by Emerson. Dickinson herself received what she called "a beautiful copy" of Emerson's *Poems* in 1850 from her friend Ben Newton, and she found them to be "very pleasant" (L 30). Emerson gave lectures in Amherst on at least two occasions, and there is no reason to believe that Emily did not hear him speak, according to Richard Sewall, who considers Emerson as a major influence on Dickinson. It is significant to note in this context that when Dickinson's poem "Success is counted sweetest" (P 67) was published anonymously in 1878, it was attributed by more than one critic to Emerson. Conversely, Emerson's poem "The House" has been designated as one of Dickinson's because it is so similar to her poetry in rhythm, content, and musical terminology. In this poem Emerson wrote, "She lays her beams in music / In music every one, / To the cadence of the whirling world / Which dances round the sun." In his essay "The Poet," Emerson claimed that "whenever we are so finely organized that we can penetrate into that region where the air is music, we hear those primal warblings and attempt to write them down...." Who is to say that these thoughts did not serve as the inspiration for Dickinson's poem "Musicians wrestle everywhere — / All day — among the crowded air / I hear the silver strife —" (P 157). Emerson's musical influence on Dickinson may have been quite extensive, and a comparative analysis is warranted. At the very least, it can be said with certainty that the two poets were "musically" in tune.

Dickinson's musical affinities with Emerson's protégé Henry David Thoreau are more obscure, yet her few intriguing allusions to Thoreau indicate a relationship greater than she ever acknowledged. A copy of *Walden,* with markings attributed to Dickinson, was in the library at the Homestead, and it seems entirely plausible that Dickinson read and took to heart this now famous passage from the conclusion of *Walden:*

> If a man does not keep pace with his companions, perhaps it is because he hears a different drummer. Let him step to the music which he hears, however measured or far away.

These words relate most appropriately to those spoken by Emily Dickinson's friend and editor, Mabel Loomis Todd, in her preface to *Poems by Emily Dickinson, Second Series:* "Emily Dickinson's verses all show a strange cadence of inner rhythmical music ... appealing, indeed to an unrecognized sense more elusive than hearing."

Though the two women never met face-to-face, Todd "penetrated, ultimately, to the 'real' Emily Dickinson more surely than did any of Emily's close associates."[2] Their friendship was founded and nurtured on their mutual love of music. Todd, a gifted musician, frequently came to the Homestead to play and sing for Emily, who heard every note, though she never entered the drawing room but remained, instead, in the dark hall or on the stairs. Todd recorded that she "usually sang to Emily for an hour or more, playing afterwards selections from Beethoven and Bach or Scarlatti, which she admired almost extravagantly."[3] After Todd finished each recital, Dickinson always sent her "a glass of wine on a silver salver, and with it either a piece of cake or a rose — and a poem, the latter usually impromptu, evidently written on the spot."[4]

Their shared passion for music made Todd uniquely suited to include in her editorial comments to *The Letters of Emily Dickinson* (1894) that "Music had always charm for Emily Dickinson." That charm began when Dickinson, at age two and a half, played what she called "the moosic" on her Aunt Lavinia's piano, and it lasted until her final years, when she listened from the top of the stairway at the Homestead to the music of invited guests. In the intervening years, music served not only as a source of pleasure but as a source of inspiration for the writing of both her prose and her poetry. It is from these two writings, and from the letters of family and friends, that we find evidence of Dickinson's musical knowledge and talent.

Among Dickinson's earliest letters are those she wrote to her friend Abiah Root. Though these letters contain material on subjects appropriate to girls of their age, they clearly emphasize their common interest in music and their mutual progress on the piano. Both girls used a popular instructional book of the day, *Bertini's Piano Method Complete*, which was a progressive and complete method for the pianoforte, specifically designed to challenge pupils to exert themselves and to familiarize them with all the difficulties of tonality, fingering, and rhythm. Inspection of this book in the Dickinson Collection at the Jones Library in Amherst suggests that completion of such a study would result in exceptional musicianship, for the lessons were designed with increasing difficulty from the natural key up to those most charged with chromatic signs. In his preface, Henri Bertini acknowledges that his system will necessarily give considerable trouble to pupils at the outset, but from it, he says, "there will afterwards result a great good to them—for, in learning to play the Piano-Forte, they will, at the same time, become good musicians." In a letter to Root, Dickinson, reporting on her progress in Bertini's book, says that she is "getting along in it very well. Aunt Selby says she shant let me have many tunes now for she wants I should get over in the book a good ways first" (L 7). Dickinson's dedication to practice and her desire to progress surely indicate her desire to become a fine musician.

Edward Dickinson may well have recognized his daughter's musical talent, and he must have known of her desire for a piano, for, as

Emily wrote Abiah on May 7, 1845, "Father intends to have a piano very soon. How happy I shall be when I have one of my own!" (L 6). The search for that special piano began in a letter her father wrote to Emily on June 4, 1844, while she was visiting the William Dickinson family in Worcester: "Tell Uncle William that I want a Piano when he can buy good ones, at a fair price. I hope he & Mr. Leland will go to Boston, this week, & find two good ones. I prefer *Rosewood*—3 pedals—& a stool. I want all together."[5]

It was nearly a year later, when Emily was fourteen years old, that she finally had a piano of her own, and what a beautiful instrument it was! It is now in the Emily Dickinson Room of the Houghton Library at Harvard University, and it is truly a grand, ornate, and remarkably beautiful piano. Made by Hallet Davis & Company of Boston, it is a very large rosewood piano with heavy, deeply carved legs. Intricate wooden decorations adorn both the legs and the wooden area below the keyboard. The piano stool which Edward Dickinson requested is of the pedestal type with a red velvet top. Emily's father enjoyed hearing her play this magnificent piano, and, on her first visit home from Mount Holyoke Seminary, Emily records, "Father wishing to hear the Piano, I like an obedient daughter, played & sang a few tunes, much to his apparent gratification" (L 20).

Hours and hours of practice went into producing piano music that would please her father. In September of 1845, Emily writes Abiah that she is taking piano lessons and getting along very well with them, adding, "… and now I have a piano, I am very happy" (L 8). She was still taking piano lessons in January of 1846 and practicing two hours every day, a discipline she continued throughout the summer of 1846. When she returned from a visit to Boston too late to enter Amherst Academy for the fall term, she put her time to good use nonetheless, "sewing, practicing upon the piano, and assisting Mother in household affairs" (L 14). She maintained her musical interests while she was a student at Mount Holyoke Seminary in 1847–1848, where her daily activities, which included a heavy academic load, consisted of one-half hour of singing in Seminary Hall and one hour of practicing on the piano. Dickinson's consistent and dedicated piano practice sessions, along with her piano lessons through the years, provided her with the solid musical background required to become a fine pianist.

The much admired

SLIDING WALTZ.

BOSTON: Published by C. H. KEITH 67 & 69 Court St.

Examination of Emily Dickinson's personal, bound volume of miscellaneous sheet music at the Houghton Library at Harvard confirms that she did, indeed, become a highly accomplished pianist. She played the popular waltzes of the day, and her album contains arrangements of nine of them attributed to Beethoven; a piece entitled "Home as Waltz"; and "Sounds from Home, A Set of Waltzes." Three other waltzes should be mentioned because of their ranking order of difficulty. "The Bird Waltz for the Harp or Piano Forte" is a difficult piece; "Aurora Waltz" is classed as very difficult; and "Sliding Waltz" could only be played by an accomplished musician, for it is exceptionally difficult. In order to play this waltz, a musician would need mastery of the "slide" run, as well as the skill to make these runs flow in rhythm, for in some cases there are seven notes to the beat, in others nine, and in some cases six notes to the beat. "Sliding Waltz" would require excellent musical coordination and sense of timing.

Dickinson played the popular quick steps and marches of the day such as "Louisville March and Quick Step," "Home Quick Step," "March and Quick Step in the Battle of Prague," "The Lancer's Quick Step," and "Wood Up, A Quick Step," but these did not require unusual skill, though they would have been entertaining pieces to play at parties and home gatherings. Her arrangement of "Home, Sweet Home," a favorite tune of the day, would have been suited to social situations similar to those where the waltzes and quick steps were played.

Many of the pieces of music in Dickinson's Portfolio of Music fall into the category of "salon music," which was music designed for pleasurable entertaining in home parlors or salons. This type of music included favorite melodies transcribed into variations, which was a very traditional way to elongate the enjoyment of a favorite melody by presenting the melody in varied styles, tempos, flowing embellishments, and keys. They were often written to give the impression of requiring greater ability than the piece actually demanded. Many well-known nineteenth-century composers wrote salon music because of the lucrative market salon sheet music provided for them.

Dickinson's portfolio contained a number of these salon pieces. However, her selections did require proficiency; her sheets of salon music not only look difficult, they are difficult, for they contain many intricate and complicated variations on popular songs of the times which would be challenging for the majority of pianists. For example, her arrangement of "Believe Me If All Those Endearing Young Charms" would require excellent agility in melismatic passages in the right hand throughout and extraordinary agility in order to attain fluidity in all the running passages. In "Auld Lang Syne with Variations for the Piano Forte or Harp," the melody is in the right hand embellished with lots of ornamentation around it, with the basic chord structure outlining it in the left hand. In each variation within the piece, the melody is distinct, but the embellishment is different with different musical characteristics in each one. Measured trills and turns add to its difficulty.

One final salon piece should be noted for its intricate, convoluted style. "Di Tanti Palpiti, A Favorite Air from *Tancredi* with Variations for the Piano Forte" was a mezzo-soprano aria in the opera *Tancredi* by Rossini. It was known throughout Europe and was widely considered to be the most popular opera aria of its time. Dickinson's copy of this piece would be considered quite challenging because it demands fingering agility and fluidity of the right hand for the runs and because it has numerous rhythmic changes. Without a doubt, it would take advanced proficiency at the piano to play many of the pieces of music in Dickinson's portfolio. Years of piano lessons and practice, as well as good flexibility in the fingers, would be requirements for playing such music and for accomplishing such extraordinary musical challenges. Although her sister Lavinia (known to her family and friends as Vinnie) played the piano also, there can be no doubt that Emily was *the* musician at the Homestead.

The disparity in the sisters' musical ability is indicated in an exchange of letters between Emily and Austin. In the first letter, dated November 16, 1851, Emily thanks her brother for sending a piece of music, a duet for the girls to play together, and adds confidently, "I shall learn my part of the Duett, and try to have Vinnie her's [*sic*]" (L 65). Two months later, Emily writes Austin, reminding him that he sent them the Duett, but she states quite frankly, "Vinnie cannot learn it, and I see from the outside page, that there is a piece for *two* hands. Are you willing to change it" (L 71). Without question, the bound volume of sheet music from the Homestead contains music

"Di Tanti Palpiti, a Favorite Air from *Tancredi* with Variations for the Piano Forte"

"Believe Me If All Those Endearing Young Charms"

"Auld Lang Syne with Variations for the Piano Forte or Harp"

which only Emily could have played, and any doubts about her musicianship can be negated by viewing her repertoire of piano pieces.

Dickinson's ability to play these demanding pieces evidently resulted from her early, solid musical instruction by the Bertini method. However, Henri Bertini acknowledged that even a skillful master could not give *style* to a pupil, for, he said, "Style is something that cannot be transferred, and for which no rules are given.... Style is the spirit of the performance; it is the art of giving a form to the ideas, and of transmitting feelings. It is a quality with which nature alone can gift certain intellects."

It is clear that Dickinson was one of those whom nature gifted, for, after mastering the elements of piano instruction, she developed a distinctive and creative style of her own. Her friend Kate Scott Anthon later recalled "those blissful evenings at Austin's" when "Emily was often at the piano playing weird & beautiful melodies, all from her own inspiration...."[6] Dickinson's cousin John Graves often stayed at the Homestead as protector for the Dickinson women while Squire Dickinson served as a Representative in Washington, and Graves' daughter has left an important account of his impression of Emily's music: "Oftentimes, during those visits to the Dickinson relatives, father would be awakened from his sleep by heavenly music. Emily would explain in the morning, 'I can improvise better at night.'"[7] In a letter to John, Dickinson recalls those memories of "heavenly music" when she writes: "I play the old, odd tunes yet, which used to flit about your head after honest hours — and wake dear Sue, and madden me, with their grief and fun —" (L 184). These "old, odd tunes" were distinctly those of her own making, and there can be little doubt that Dickinson found creative expression in her improvisational melodies, expression which would eventually spill over into her poetic endeavors.

In addition to her own piano "concerts," Dickinson attended numerous musical events and made perceptive evaluations of each one. She writes Abiah Root about the performance of a Chinese musician at the Chinese Museum in Boston: "The Musician played upon two of his instruments & accompanied them with his voice." Unfamiliar with the sounds of what was then called Oriental music, Dickinson admits, "It needed great command over my risible faculty to enable me to keep sober as this amateur was performing, yet he was so very polite to give us some of his native music that we could not do otherwise than to express ourselves highly edified by his performance" (L 13). On another occasion, Emily and Vinnie attended a Germanian Concert with their cousin John Graves and in a letter to her brother Austin describing the event, Emily claims that she "never heard such *sounds* before." To her, the German band "seemed like *brazen Robins* all wearing broadcloth wings, and I think they were, for they all flew away as soon as the concert was over" (L 118).

Dickinson's most thorough critique of a musical concert by far was on the celebrated Jennie Lind, known as the "Swedish Nightingale" because of her remarkably sympathetic voice of great compass, purity, control, and flexibility. Lind's brilliant career in opera and on the concert stage throughout Europe preceded her arrival in New York on September 1, 1850, and according to Millicent Todd Bingham's account in *Emily Dickinson's Home*, Jennie Lind's presence in America provided "the thrill of the moment. The response of the public to her first concert in Castle Garden on September 11 had been fantastic.... The rush to hear her turned into a stampede. In Boston, where she gave a concert on September 28, she created a 'furor.'"[8] Though Lind intended to return to Sweden the following summer, her plans were changed and she remained in America for another year, returning to Boston in June of 1851 for a series of five "farewell" concerts. Austin Dickinson attended one of these concerts in Boston and shared his impressions of Jennie Lind in a letter to his sister Emily. Likewise, in a letter to Austin on July 6, 1851, Emily wrote of the reactions she experienced when the entire Dickinson family attended the concert Jennie Lind gave at the old Edwards Church in Northampton. She described "how Jennie came out like a child and sang and sang again, how boquets fell in showers, and the roof was rent with applause — how it thundered outside, and inside with the thunder of God and of men — judge ye which was the loudest" (L 46). Continuing her commentary, Emily wrote:

> ... how we all loved Jennie Lind, but not accustomed oft to her manner of singing did'nt fancy *that* so well as we did *her* — no

doubt it was very fine — but take some notes from her 'Echo' — the Bird sounds from the 'Bird Song' and some of her curious trills, and I'd rather have a Yankee. *Herself*, and not her music, was what we seemed to love —

This description of the concert reveals much about Dickinson's preference to see "New Englandly" and could possibly have been her inspiration for "The Robin's my Criterion for Tune —" (P 285) which she would compose some ten years later.

Dickinson's most emotional response to a professional musician can be attributed to the Russian pianist Anton Rubinstein, whose performances throughout Europe and America made him the most famous pianist of his time. He toured Europe with the greatest imaginable success in 1867–70, and in 1872–73 gave 215 concerts in America from which he earned $40,000. Audiences everywhere received his playing with enthusiasm. It is clear that Dickinson shared this enthusiasm for Rubinstein's music and that she was extremely moved by it, as she expresses in this letter to her cousin Frances Norcross in late May of 1873: "Glad you heard Rubinstein. Grieved Loo could not hear him. He makes me think of polar nights Captain Hall could tell! Going from ice to ice! What an exchange of awe!" (L 390). It is possible that Dickinson's poem, "The fascinating chill that music leaves" (P 1480), had its origin in the Rubinstein music which had "chilled" her so. Years later, Clara Green, Dickinson's cousin, shared this quite revealing anecdote: "Emily told us of her early love for the piano and confided that, after hearing Rubinstein [?] —I believe it was Rubinstein—play in Boston, she had become convinced that she could never master the art and had forthwith abandoned it once and for all, giving herself up then wholly to literature."[9]

From the disciplined study of music to the creative development of her musical talent, it was but a short, metaphoric leap into the combined disciplines of music and poetry in her creative verse. As early as April of 1862, Dickinson had written to Higginson that "the noise in the Pool, at Noon — excels my Piano." (L 261), indicating Dickinson's growing awareness that the music of nature might, indeed, supersede that of the man-made, instrumental variety.

This transition signaled a subsequent outpouring of musical

imagery and musical references in Dickinson's poems and in her letters. By conservative count, 160 poems and 131 letters contain musical terminology, with multiple references to music often appearing in numerous selections. The sheer magnitude of these numbers in itself provides motivation for critical examination, and Chapter II focuses exclusively on the portions of Dickinson's poems and letters in which music plays an integral part. Analysis of these works reveals that musical imagery was a method by which Dickinson could express both her highest joys and her deepest depressions, as well as communicate some of her most profound relationships. Dickinson learned to interweave music with her poetry and her prose in such a way that it becomes a literary strategy of major consequence.

Public recognition of the overall musical quality of Dickinson's verse is evident in the numerous newspaper and magazine articles appearing after the 1890 publication of *Poems by Emily Dickinson, First Series*. Response during the last decade of the nineteenth century to the musicality of these poems remained consistent throughout the successive publications of her poetry, and attention focused on Dickinson's letters as well, when they were first seen by the reading public in 1894. Comments and literary reviews about Dickinson's works were conscientiously kept by Mabel Todd in clipping scrapbooks during the eighteen-nineties. Almost one hundred years later, Willis J. Buckingham's research has yielded numerous other documents which, added to Todd's, comprise vital primary source materials about public perceptions of music in Dickinson's poems and letters. Chapter III is devoted exclusively to analyzing these documents for what they reveal about nineteenth-century attitudes regarding the musical quality and form, or lack of them, in Dickinson's verse.

Nineteenth-century readers would have been astounded to learn that over half of Dickinson's poems and many of her letters had been locked away in a chest where they had been placed by Dickinson's first editor, Mabel Loomis Todd, following a legal dispute with Lavinia Dickinson over a parcel of land. This chest remained locked until 1929 when Todd's daughter, Millicent Todd Bingham, opened it at her mother's request. Bingham's awe at the discovery of the chest's contents is evident in her description of the event:

> All these papers were packed in a camphor-wood chest. The lock, as you turn the key, plays a little tune…. With thumping heart, I turned the key and for the first time heard that little tune.

How appropriate that a little tune played when the key turned in the lock, for some of Dickinson's finest poems relating to music were found in the chest, such as "Better — than Music! For I — who heard it —" (P 503) and "Bind me — I still can sing —" (P 1005). These and over 650 previously unpublished poems were edited by Mrs. Bingham and published in 1945 under the title *Bolts of Melody*.

These words are taken from Poem 505, in which Dickinson refers to the rare privilege of being a poet, and the last two lines read, "Had I the Art to stun myself / With Bolts of Melody!" The entire last line as Dickinson wrote it is highly significant for, by including the preposition "with," the phrase is expanded to indicate process and action, factors which are crucial to the context of this book. For it is with personal knowledge and experience in music and with musical imagery throughout her prose and poetry that Dickinson indeed "stuns" her readers "With Bolts of Melody!"

Though most of the nineteenth-century critics did not perceive it, Dickinson's melodic "Bolts" were not only contained in a form, but in a musical form, at that. Dickinson took the Protestant hymn form and made it her own, and Chapter IV concentrates on contemporary critical analysis of Dickinson's use of the hymn-tune as it provides structure, organization, and the occasion for doctrinal irony in her verse.

Poetry is a composition of words set to music, according to Ezra Pound, who claims that all poets compose verse to some sort of tune. This was a practice and skill Dickinson developed when she was quite young. In an early letter, Dickinson tells how she would sit in church thinking of her friend Sue, composing new words to the old hymns, an activity which foreshadowed the composition of the majority of her poems later on. The hymn-tune provided the bridge to Dickinson's musical verse, and "it is time to recognize music as an essential part of the architectonics of her poetry."[10] That the hymn is the basic influence in both the meter and the message of Dickinson's poetry is generally accepted by Dickinson scholars. Organization of some of their perceptive viewpoints in Chapter IV provides essential confirmation of this theory.

While Chapter IV discusses current critical opinions concerning the hymn form as the basic structure for Dickinson's poems, Chapter V provides examples of some nineteenth-century (or earlier) hymns which could have influenced Dickinson while she was in the process of composing her poems. By viewing the music of the hymns in close proximity to the poems themselves, it is possible to see how the meters of the hymns and the meters of her poems are essentially matched so that they appear to be perfect metric partners. Though no claim is made that these are the exact hymns which influenced Dickinson, they are all hymns which were popular in New England during her lifetime and the possibility that she knew most of them, if not all, is quite credible. Dickinson's years of attending Sabbath evening singing school and of singing in choirs at both Amherst Academy and Mount Holyoke Seminary not only "improved her voice," as she expressed to Abiah Root, but these singing groups would have introduced her to new hymns and would have reinforced familiar ones. Hymn-tunes established the meter of Dickinson's verse, and the illustrations offered in Chapter V help to clarify that concept.

Thus far this book has focused on the musical influences in Dickinson's life which later became creative strategies for expression in her poetry and letters. An analysis of Emily Dickinson and music would be incomplete, however, without considering the affective power her musical verse has had on musicians, and on composers in particular. Chapter VI focuses attention in a way previously neglected on some of the many composers who have been inspired by the musical qualities of Dickinson's work to create musical settings for her verse. This interest in Dickinson's works continues to increase in popularity among composers and arrangers.

Composers are drawn to Dickinson's poems for a variety of reasons, and some of these reasons are analyzed in Chapter VI. Personal correspondence with a selected group of composers who have set Dickinson's poetry to music provides an exciting perspective from which to view the interchange between poet and musician. No analysis of the intellectual thought and the creativity behind the merger of

Dickinson's verse with music could compare with the rare opportunity these letters afford to catch the passion of these composers for Dickinson's poetry and to present their own explanations of their particular musical setting or settings. Their letters contain a vibrant quality which I have endeavored to retain through either direct quotations or paraphrases of their thoughts and expressions. This method, used in Chapter VI, provides a significant viewpoint for witnessing musical artists at work interpreting musical verse, a vision which adds an important dimension to the vital connection existing between Emily Dickinson and music.

The intent of Dickinson scholarship should be to make her works more understandable and, as Richard Sewall says, "In our attempt to understand the workings of Dickinson's genius, no clue can be overlooked. Even the slightest detail may turn out to be important. Nothing is irrelevant."[11] The history of Dickinson scholarship exemplifies the search for clues which Sewall mentions. According to Barton Levi St. Armand, Dickinson's poems have been "so cut up, dismembered, picked over, anthologized, and selected that we are in danger of losing touch with the original sensibility that produced them."[12] Editors have sometimes arbitrarily classified Dickinson's verse into such categories as "Life," "Love," "Death," "Nature," and "Immortality," while critics have repeatedly attempted to grasp the essence of Dickinson's life and works by applying all the known tools of methodology. Divisions such as these provide focused study of individual aspects of Dickinson's verse, but, as such, do not lend unity to the canon. Perhaps only music can perform such a feat, for it permeates Dickinson's poems and letters throughout, providing emotional depth and meaning to her words. It has been said that Dickinson *thought* musically, and it is certain that for her, "music ... served as a metaphor for poetry."[13] Music is one of the vibrant strands woven into the grand design of Dickinson's collected works. To ignore the importance of its presence in her poetry and letters is to lose sight of one of Dickinson's most artistic and creative strategies.

CHAPTER II

Musical Imagery in Dickinson's Poems and Letters

Music is a vital element in Emily Dickinson's poetry. Melodic strains and musical references pervade her poems and her letters, providing unusually appropriate figurative language to express Dickinson's joyous and plaintive moods. The creative power Dickinson achieves through the use of musical imagery is undeniable, yet musical imagery as an organizing theme in her poetry and in her letters has not yet been fully explored as a major facet of Emily Dickinson's poetic genius. To an astonishing degree, the pulsating rhythms and sounds which Dickinson orchestrates in hundreds of her poems and letters testify to her rare ability to convey profound concepts in musical terminology. Indeed, sometimes the very air around her seems filled with music, and the songs of the birds either lift her exalted spirit or trouble her downcast soul. At other times, music emanates from the depths of her own being to create contrapuntal melodies which achieve either a harmonic or a dissonant whole. Dickinson's assertion, "In adequate Music there is a Major and a Minor —" (L 370), is a philosophy which she incorporates into her writing, because, whether created and developed in major keys of exhilaration or in minor keys of depression, music is one of Dickinson's most effective strategies for expressing her sensitive and provocative thoughts.

Examination of this strategy forms the basis of this chapter, which provides an overview of some of the many ways in which Dickinson calls upon musical analogies to express poetically her attitudes about relationships, nature, bird song, immortality, and emotional pain and despair. Critical approaches to these categories abound, so there is no intention to replicate those but to indicate instead the extent to which Dickinson combines music and poetry to create a distinct literary strategy of dynamic proportions. Musical imagery adds beauty, meaning, and emotional power to Dickinson's poems and letters, as the following selections indicate.

Dickinson employs musical terminology to describe some of the people whose lives were inextricably entwined with her own. One of these was Susan Gilbert Dickinson, Emily's close friend before she became her sister-in-law. In a poem honoring Susan as her other "sister," Emily acknowledges that Susan "did not sing as we did — / It was a different tune / Herself to her a music / As Bumble bee of June" (P 14). This "different tune" was evident quite often during their five decades of friendship, and, when a particularly severe rift occurred, Emily proposed a parting of the ways, suggesting, "then pass on singing Sue, and up the distant hill I journey on" (L 173).

The sudden death of Susan's eight-year-old son Gilbert was a tremendous emotional blow to "Aunt Emily," for her young nephew was especially dear to her. Her expression of grief to Susan includes this musical description of Gilbert: "His life was like the Bugle, which winds itself away, his Elegy an echo — his Requiem ecstasy —" (L 868). This tribute to Gilbert's life reflects the indelible impact he had on those who loved him.

The love affair that existed between Judge Otis P. Lord and Emily Dickinson has been well documented, but the musical connection between the two is of interest as well. The close friendship between Judge Lord and Edward Dickinson is reflected in the poem "The Judge is like the Owl – / I've heard my Father tell —," but it is Emily's voice that speaks in the last stanza, "I only ask a Tune / At Midnight — Let the Owl select / His favorite Refrain" (P 699). The interconnectedness of music in their relationship is expressed when Emily writes to Lord, "… have we not a Hymn that no one knows but us?" (L 790). Her letter to Benjamin Kimball following Judge Lord's death once again underscores the musical quality of the love affair between the two: "He did not tell me he 'sang' to you, though to sing in his presence was involuntary, thronged only with Music, like the Decks of Birds" (L 968). Judge Lord's death prompted Dickinson's observation that "Abstinence from Melody was what made him die" (L 968), indicating her contention that melody is all but essential to the life force itself.

The expansiveness of Dickinson's musical thought is indicated in her belief that "The earth has many keys. / Where melody is not / Is the unknown peninsula." (P 1775). Dickinson's atypical use of periods here emphasizes her conviction about the vital importance of melody in the world. Even ordinary relationships are enhanced by melody, according to Dickinson, who describes time spent with friends as "those melodious moments of which friends are composed" (L 969). When she writes of the comfortable relationship shared by her father and his law associate Howland, she observes that "they go along as smoothly as friendly barks at sea — or when harmonious stanzas become one melody" (L 52). In expressing her sense that speechless sympathy often excels the vocal form of remembrance, she states that "The words the happy say / Are paltry melody / But those the silent feel / Are beautiful —" (P 1750). Though she writes descriptively of "a dateless — Melody" (P 297); "That phraseless Melody —" (P 321); "Dirks of Melody" (P 1420); and "cautious melody" (P 1084); she is unable to define the word itself, recognizing that "The Definition of Melody — is — / That Definition is none — / " (P 797). Nonetheless, she senses the permanence of melody, as she expresses in Poem 1578:

> Blossoms will run away,
> Cakes reign but a Day,
> But Memory like Melody
> Is pink Eternally.

This eternal quality of melody infuses the two worlds in which Dickinson seems to co-exist, those of Nature and Immortality, and her poems and letters on these two great "Flood" subjects are liberally sprinkled with melody.

"Nature is Harmony —" (P 668), according to Dickinson, and her variant word *melody* for *harmony* indicates the extent to which she senses the musical harmony of nature. In this respect, Dickinson may have been influenced by the following thoughts Thomas Carlyle expressed in *Heroes and Hero Worship*, a book in the Dickinson library which contains markings considered to be Emily Dickinson's:

> All deep things are Song. It seems somehow the very central essence of us, Song; as if all the rest were but wrappings and hulls! ... The Greeks fabled of Sphere-Harmonies: it was the feeling they had of the inner structure of Nature; that the soul of all her voices and utterances was perfect music. Poetry, therefore, we will call *musical Thought*. The Poet is he who *thinks* in that manner.... See deep enough, and you see musically; the heart of Nature *being* everywhere music, if you can only reach it.[1]

The literary critic Higginson indicated the depth of Dickinson's kinship with nature when he concluded, "... in dealing with Nature she often seems to possess a sixth sense." With this "sixth sense," Dickinson is able to discern the sounds of nature as the harmonious music of "'the Spheres' — at play!", and for her, "Musicians wrestle everywhere — / All day — among the crowded air / I hear the silver strife —" (P 157). Dickinson's verse exemplifies what Thomas Carlyle expressed in his thoughts on the interconnectedness of poetry, music, and nature. She is definitely in tune with the music of nature as she expresses in Poem 1373:

> The worthlessness of Earthly things
> The Ditty is that Nature Sings —
> And then — enforces their delight
> Till Synods are inordinate —

Many of Dickinson's poems and letters are canticles of praise for the beautiful world and for the marvelous creatures in it. She sees the world as a tantalizingly awesome habitation for God's creatures, who live according to established and regulated plans. These creatures are occupied with the process of playing or the business of living, which in itself brings pleasure to them, for, as Dickinson observes, "Work might be electric Rest / To those that Magic make —" (P 1585). It is through musical terminology that Dickinson regularly describes the activities of these creatures. She often writes of the bee's music, as in this letter to an unknown recipient: "Wonder stings me more than the Bee — who did never sting me — but made gay music with his might wherever I did go" (L 248). In a brief, but accurate description of the brevity of popular acclaim, she asserts, "Fame is a bee. / It has a song — / It has a sting — / Ah, too, it has a wing." (P 1763). In a letter to Mrs. J. G. Holland, Dickinson inquires about her "little Byron," who, like the English poet, had a congenital defect in the tendons of one foot, expressing the hope that he "gains his foot without losing his genius — as the bee's prong and his song are concomitant" (L 227). And, in a letter to Higginson, Dickinson comments on his brief visit of December 3, 1873: "Of your flitting coming it is fair to think. Like the Bee's Coupe — vanishing in Music" (L 405). For Dickinson, the bee's "Labor is a Chant" and "His Idleness — a Tune —" (P 916), and when bees proclaim the flower they prefer, they do so "In sovereign — Swerveless Tune —" (P 380).

Dickinson focuses on the music of other creatures in numerous whimsical ways. To Mrs. Samuel Bowles she writes, "The Frogs sing sweet — today —" (L 262), and she closes a letter to Mrs. Holland with, "Good Night — I am going to sleep if the Rat permit me — I hear him singing now to the Tune of a Nut" (L 370). Dickinson informs her Norcross cousins that "Maggie's hens are warbling" (L 690), and she writes them that "Tabby is singing *Old Hundred*, which, by the way, is her maiden name" (L 410).

Musical themes centering around nature are prevalent in Dickinson's letters to her brother Austin while he was attending law school at Harvard. In an early letter, she relates to him that the breakfast is so warm and "pussy is here a singing and the tea kettle sings too as if to see which was loudest and I am so afraid lest kitty should be beaten" (L 58). Dickinson missed her brother dreadfully during his years away, and she often wrote to him about his empty room at the Homestead. In one letter, she reports that his room is "snug and cozy thro' these chilly evenings" and "the stove is singing the merry song of the wood" (L 60). In another, she describes the lonely look of his room and claims that she is going "to set out *Crickets* as soon as I find time that their shrill singing shall help disperse the gloom" (L 43). Dickinson grants crickets special powers, for she begins Poem 1104 in this way: "The Crickets sang / And set the Sun."

Dickinson is extremely responsive to the cricket's song, and she often associates important memories with it. After her friend Emily Fowler Ford moved away, Dickinson wrote her of a deep desire to see her "at twilight sitting in the door — and I shall when the leaves fall, sha'n't I, and the crickets begin to sing?" (L 161). Dickinson seems to mark the passage of time in this way, for she tells her cousin John Graves how lonely it is without him and how they all miss him, yet she thinks they will miss him even more "when a year from now comes, and the crickets sing" (L 170). And in a September 1884 letter to Mrs. Holland she writes, "Autumn is among us, though almost unperceived — and the Cricket sings in the morning, now, a most pathetic conduct" (L 936). Dickinson expresses this thought in a poem she sent to Higginson which she entitled "My Cricket": "Further in Summer than the Birds / Pathetic from the Grass / A minor Nation celebrates / Its unobtrusive Mass" (P 1068).

Even flies provide music for Dickinson. While Vinnie is visiting their cousin Louise Norcross, Dickinson writes a letter to them, one intended to emphasize how much she misses Vinnie at home. To combat her boredom, she claims to be entertained by a fly — "a timid creature, that hops from pane to pane of her white house, so very cheerfully, and hums and thrums, a sort of speck piano" (L 206). In a distinctly different and more somber mood, Dickinson writes of another fly in the poem "I heard a Fly buzz — when I died —" whose "Blue—uncertain stumbling Buzz —" interposed "Between the light — and me —" (P 465). Here the fly does not entertain but rather becomes the focal point through which the poet expresses by synaesthesia the point of view of one whose senses are breaking down. The expression of these diverse moods indicates Dickinson's ability to employ musical terminology for heightened, imagistic effect in both her letters and her poetry.

Music also becomes a means by which Dickinson describes some of the powerful forces of nature. Lightning, for instance, causes no concern when he "playeth —," she says, but "when He singeth" in "short-sepulchral Bass" (P 630), the poet finds cause for alarm. Dickinson finds music in the wind, as well. When it gently passes by, it simply stirs the grass "all day to pretty Tunes / The Breezes fetch along —" (P 333),[2] but when it becomes a stormy wind, it can "rock the Grass / With threatening Tunes and low —" (P 824). As the wind passes, its "Fingers / Let go a music — as of tunes / Blown tremulous in Glass —" (P 436), and when it gains momentum, martial imagery describes the "pompous" wind stepping "to incorporeal Tunes," clarifying the scenery and correcting errors of the sky (P 1418). When the wind increases to even greater intensity, "The Trees like Tassels — hit — and swung —," generating the rise of "a Tune / From Miniature Creatures / Accompanying the Sun —" (P 606). When Dickinson's spirits are low, she finds that "the orchestra of winds perform their strange, sad music" (L 60), but the wind can also exalt the poet and bring her great pleasure. The musical imagery of Poem 321 becomes the remarkable means by which Dickinson describes the wind's sounds as it gives her immense delight by playing its "phraseless Melody" in the "Boughs" of trees. Here she presents the voice of the wind as it forms a "Caravan of Sound" which moves through the trees and plays them, measure for measure, like a piece of piano music:

> Of all the Sounds despatched abroad,
> There's not a Charge to me
> Like that old measure in the Boughs —
> That phraseless Melody —
> The Wind does — working like a Hand,
> Whose fingers Comb the Sky —
> Then quiver down — with tufts of Tune —
> Permitted Gods, and me —
>
> . . . .
>
> When Winds go round and round in Bands —
> And thrum upon the door,
> And Birds take places, overhead,
> To bear them Orchestra.

In this poem, Dickinson speaks of "Bands" and an "Orchestra," and she was well qualified to do so, for she was keenly aware of the basic functions of the musical instruments which are used in these groups, and she found creative and imaginative ways to incorporate these stringed, wind, and percussion instruments into her poems and letters. Dickinson uses the word "Band" quite appropriately in three poems. In one instance, unable to describe an exhilarating experience she had, she attempts to do so by saying that the occasion was *not* "'Band' — in brass and scarlet — drest" (P 157). In another, the birds, who had begun singing at four o'clock with "A Music numerous as space —" ceased singing by six without a fanfare of any kind, "And yet the Band was gone —" (P 783). In a poem based on school terminology and mathematical equations, Dickinson relates the unquestionable value and equality the Heavenly Father places on each individual "Student," regarding "least Cypherer alike / With Leader of the Band" (P 545). And, in an attempt to express the stimulating effect her Norcross cousins have on her seemingly uneventful life, Dickinson writes to them, "When I think of your little faces I feel as the band does before it makes its first shout…" (L 344).

A band consists mostly of wind and percussion instruments, and Dickinson is particularly partial to these instruments in her poems. She often speaks of the drum, the oldest musical instrument, one that expresses the ancient, instinctive love of rhythm. "I love the Drums," Dickinson claims in an 1884 letter to Mrs. J. G. Holland, adding, "and they are busy now" (L 950), indicating the activities surrounding the coming Election Day. Twenty years before, while she was in Cambridge for medical treatment, she wrote to Vinnie that "The Drums keep on for the still Man, but Emily must stop" (L 297), a reference perhaps to Abraham Lincoln's visit to Cambridge which included a torchlight parade. Dickinson often associates drums with military imagery, as she does in a letter to Abiah Root, which describes a great temptation she has overcome and conquered, "not a glorious victory, where you hear the rolling drum, but a kind of helpless victory, where triumph would come of itself, faintest music…" (L 36). In the nightmarish experience the poet relates in "I dreaded that first Robin, so," creatures of Nature pass by her in revue, "Each one salutes me, as he goes, / And I, my childish Plumes, / Lift, in bereaved acknowledgment / Of their unthinking Drums —" (P 348). In a poem depicting a military funeral, the poet finds she has been caught up in the glory of the occasion, but her "Triumph lasted till the Drums / Had left the Dead alone / And then I dropped my Victory" (P 1227). She finds that pomp and pageantry can have a piercing quality, for "Music's triumphant — / But the fine Ear / Winces with delight / Are Drums too near —" (P 582).

In a number of poems, Dickinson combines percussion and wind instruments, as she does in "Awake ye muses nine, sing me a strain divine" (P 1), where she presumably suggests to her Valentine, "And bring the fife, and trumpet, and beat upon the drum / ." In a poem with Civil War overtones, Dickinson writes of the agony of defeat when she says, "My Portion is Defeat — today / A paler luck than Victory — / Less Paeans — fewer Bells — / The Drums don't follow Me — with tunes," yet, "over there," where there is "Victory," she finds, "The Trumpets tell it to the Air —" (P 639). Dickinson employs martial music to depict some decidedly religious poems, as well. In one, which praises the martyrs who have suffered until, in "God's full time," they are taken to their reward, the poet finds power in their examples, saying, "That I — grown bold — / Step martial — at my Crucifixion — / As Trumpets — rolled — / Feet, small as mine — have marched in Revolution / Firm to the Drum —" (P 295). In "Over and over, like a Tune," she again speaks in military terms of how "The Recollection plays — " of "Drums off the Phantom Battlements / Cornets of Paradise — " which give "Snatches" and "Cadences" from "Baptized Generations" who are "at the Lord's Right hand" (P 367). In another poem, the poet describes how dream visions allow her to enter into "parlors, shut by day," where she meets with her "King, who does not speak —." So vivid are these heavenly dreams that when the morning comes, "It is as if a hundred drums / Did round my pillow roll, / And shouts fill all my Childish sky, / And Bells keep saying 'Victory' / From steeples in my soul!" (P 103). And, finally, Dickinson's most familiar use of the drum is found in "I felt a Funeral, in my Brain," where, when all the mourners are seated, "A Service, like a Drum — / Kept beating — beating — till I thought / My Mind was going numb —." The percussion quality of the drum, with the shock of its repetitious sound waves on the ear, could scarcely be conveyed more sensitively. Then, the poet adds, "Space — began to toll, / As all the Heavens were a Bell, / And Being, but an Ear" (P 280). The power of this poem depends on the impact which these two percussion instruments make on the psychically fragile speaker of the poem.

For Dickinson, the trumpet, a treble brass wind instrument, is generally associated with things eternal, as evidenced in this letter

Emily wrote to her sister-in-law Susan, who had come to the Homestead to visit, but no one had let her in: "I would have come out of Eden to open the Door for you if I had known you were there — You must knock with a Trumpet as Gabriel does, whose Hands are small as yours —" (L 662). And in one of her earliest poems, "Sic transit gloria mundi," Dickinson writes of the forefathers who died at Bunker Hill long ago and are sleeping there still but, "The trumpet, sir, shall wake them, / In dreams I see them rise, / Each with a solemn musket / A marching to the skies!" (P 3). Dickinson's belief in future recognition, and even fame, after death is expressed in these lines, "There is no Trumpet like the Tomb," when "the sweet Acclamation of Death" (L 1043) reveals that which has yet been unknown.

The bugle, another treble wind instrument, most often becomes the precursor to death in Dickinson's poems. In one poem, winds go "To their Ethereal Homes / Whose Bugles call the least of us / To undepicted Realms" (P 1634), and in another poem, "Death is the supple Suitor," who woos "By pallid innuendoes / And dim approach" but who eventually wins, "brave at last with Bugles" (P 1445). In a sympathy letter to Mrs. Edward Tuckerman over the death of a loved one, Dickinson writes, "Corinthians' Bugle obliterates the Birds, so cover your loved Heart to keep it from another shot" (L 1020). Here Dickinson refers to the day of resurrection recorded in I Corinthians 15:52 when "the trumpet shall sound, and the dead shall be raised incorruptible, and we shall all be changed." And in a letter expressing lamentation over the "Death Bed of a young Flower to which I was deeply attached," Dickinson adds, "The element of Elegy, like Bugles at a Grave, how solemnly inspiriting!" (L 945). Dickinson also uses the bugle in a military context, referring to the Civil War, in a letter to Helen Hunt Jackson. After expressing thanks for Mrs. Jackson's concern for her health, Dickinson asserts, "Who could be ill in March, that Month of proclamation? Sleigh Bells and Jays contend in my Matinee, and the North surrenders, instead of the South, a reverse of Bugles" (L 976).

Dickinson incorporates the pipe organ into two poems, both of which reflect the profound impression the music of this largest and most powerful musical instrument produces in her. In one of the poems, the organ's "talk," which is its music, produces a breath-taking reaction in the speaker, as Poem 183 indicates: "I've heard an Organ talk, sometimes / In a Cathedral Aisle / And understood no word it said — / Yet held my breath, the while —," and though she does not comprehend why the music has made such an impact, she goes away purer for having heard it. The poet expresses an opposite response to organ music in Poem 258 which compares the sensation "a certain Slant of light" engenders on "Winter Afternoons — " to the oppression that "the Heft / Of Cathedral Tunes" (heavy, ponderous pipe organ music) can produce within an individual, leaving a sensation of "Heavenly Hurt" within, "Where the meanings, are —." Here, as in so many of Dickinson's poems, the perception of similar experiences is subject to change, depending on the receptivity of the individual at any given time.

In Dickinson's hands, the flute, a treble wood-wind instrument, becomes a means to describe bird song, a poet, and a game. In the first instance, the poet writes about the appearance of a small, inconspicuous "Carnation" which would not be noted at all, except for the fact that its quiet appearance brings "Our little garden that we lost / Back to the Lawn again" (P 81). With the appearance of this harbinger of spring, bees buzz drunkenly about and "silver steal a hundred flutes / From out a hundred trees —," as the birds contribute their music to this early springtime scene. Another poem, a eulogy for Dickinson's favorite woman poet, Elizabeth Barrett Browning, declares that with her death, "Poets — ended — / Silver — perished — with her Tongue — / Not on Record — bubbled other, / Flute — or Woman — / So divine —" (P 312). To associate the flute with her most admired poet indicates the high regard Dickinson had for this musical instrument. Another poem expresses both the renunciation of and the desire for the speaker to live with her loved one and to perform every imaginable act that would bring him satisfaction and pleasure. The joy it would bring her to comply with "His weariest Commandment —" would be "sweeter to obey, / Than 'Hide and Seek' — / Or skip to Flutes — / Or All Day, chase the Bee —" (P 366). These childhood games which once brought pleasure have been replaced with a deep desire to serve her beloved. In this same poem, the speaker aspires to play "his chosen tune — / On Lute the least — the latest —" for whatever delights him would be her joy to give.

The lute is an ancient stringed instrument which was most

popular in the 1500s and 1600s, and during the next two centuries the lute came to represent poetry as well as music. Dickinson uses this musical instrument in that context in "Put up my lute! / What of — my Music! / Since the sole ear I cared to charm — / Passive — as Granite — laps My Music —" (P 261). In another poem, music is described as being within the lark, rolled in silver bulbs to be parceled out sparingly, or "Scantily dealt to the Summer Morning" so that its music will be conserved, that is, "Saved for your Ear when Lutes be old" (P 861). Dickinson finds another use for the lute in a letter to her "Dearest of all dear Uncles," Joel Warren Norcross. In this whimsical, even farcical letter upbraiding her uncle for not writing her as he promised, she tells him of a dream she had, one in which youthful men, "all strong and stout-hearted … made life one summer day — they danced to the sound of the lute — they sang old snatches of song — and they quaffed the rosy wine" (L 29). This imaginary scene has an antique quality about it, once again confirming her knowledge of the lute as an ancient instrument. She seems to maintain this concept in "A Drop fell on the Apple Tree —," a poem describing rain drops as the impetus for stimulating transitions from former states into present ones. Here she pictures a gala entertainment held outdoors where "The Birds jocoser sung —" and where "The Breezes brought dejected Lutes — / And bathed them in the Glee —" (P 794).

Dickinson made more references to bells than to any other musical instrument, and it is clear that she considered the bell to have musical and communicable qualities. She said so in Poem 1008: "How still the Bells in Steeples stand / Till swollen with the Sky / They leap upon their silver Feet / In frantic Melody!" In one poem, "There came a Wind like a Bugle —," the awesome force of the wind brings about such changes in the scenery that "The Bell within the steeple wild / The flying tidings told —" (P 1593). In 1871, Dickinson writes Louise Norcross that a "chime of bells" was given in memory of Frazar Stearns, a young Amherst man killed in the Civil War (L 362), but to her, "The mixing Bells and Palls — / Makes Lacerating Tune — To Ears the Dying Side —" (P 735). Bells could be the instruments of annunciation, as they are in the mystical poem, "There is a morn by men unseen —" where the poet awaits "thy far, fantastic bells — / Announcing me in other dells — / Unto the different dawn!" (P 24).

Dickinson also used bells to describe experiences which to her were euphoric. In one instance, she wrote Dr. and Mrs. J. G. Hollard, "I love to write to you — it gives my heart a holiday and sets the bells to ringing" (L 133). To another of her correspondents, T.W. Higginson, she described a touching incident that occurred when an "Indian Woman" came to the door of the Homestead selling "gay Baskets." Dickinson was captivated by her "dazzling Baby," who, "With jargon sweeter than a Bell, grappled Buttercups — and they sank together" (L 653). The letter in which Dickinson asks Higginson to be her "Preceptor" also contains her response to his attempts to correct her style, for she writes, "I thank you for your justice — but could not drop the Bells whose jingling cooled my Tramp" (L 265). These bells were in her soul, and they made life worth living, as she said in Poem 604, "It may be Wilderness — without — / Far feet of failing Men — / But Holiday — excludes the night — / And it is Bells — within —."

A symphony orchestra is made up mainly of stringed instruments, and these are the last to be considered here. The banjo is one of the stringed instruments Dickinson selects, for in Poem 620 she declares, "No Black bird bates his Banjo / For passing Calvary —," which indicates the total indifference of Nature to one who is suffering. The mandolin, popular for hundreds of years to accompany informal singing, produces a tone when the strings are struck with a rather stiff pick. Dickinson indicates that she understands the functions of the mandolin when she writes, "Bind me — I still can sing — / Banish — my mandolin / Strikes true within —" (P 1005). The violin is the best-known and most widely used of all stringed instruments, and three of Dickinson's poems include the violin. In one, she ponders questions about the existence of the Spirit without the Body by drawing on this musical analogy: "The Music in the Violin / Does not emerge alone / But Arm in Arm with Touch, yet Touch / Alone — is not a Tune —" (P 1576). Though she could not resolve this impenetrable conflict, the interrelationship of the violin and its music says much about her understanding of the interconnection of Spirit and Body. In "I think the longest Hour of all," the poet finds that at the highest point of anticipation her "Heart begins to crowd" and she finds herself unable to consummate her great desire. Instead, finding "her timid service done," she will "Take up my little Violin —

/ And further North — remove" (P 635). "Like Some Old fashioned Miracle" is a poem reflecting on the passage of summer and the unsuccessful attempts to recollect it. Summer's "Memories like Strains — Review — / When Orchestra is dumb — / The Violin in Baize replaced — / And Ear — and Heaven — numb —" (P 302). Finally, the guitar, one of the largest plucked string instruments, is used chiefly to accompany singing, though it can be used for almost all types of music. Dickinson found a good use for it in this short poem which exalts the music of nature and indicates that one must have an empathetic relationship with nature in order to be a true poet: "Touch lightly Nature's sweet Guitar / Unless thou know'st the Tune / Or every Bird will point at thee / Because a Bard too soon —" (P 1389).

Throughout her works, the sights and sounds of the world of nature provide the backdrop for the fascinating show God's creatures perform for her daily, a show that is "full as Opera," according to Dickinson (P 326). And it was through combined descriptions of nature and opera that Dickinson could best describe the enchantment she felt for "that Foreign Lady," Elizabeth Barrett Browning: "And just the meanest Tunes / That Nature murmured to herself / To keep herself in Cheer — / I took for Giants — practising — Titanic Opera —/ The Days — To Mighty Metres stept —" (P 593). Dickinson, indeed, found a concert of musical sounds in nature, as one of Dickinson's relatives, Clara Newman Turner, describes: "[Her] Opera was the trilling of the birds outside her window; — the buzzing of the bees; — the flitting in and out of the butterflies in their gauzy costumes. The crickets, and the frogs, and the breeze in its orchestra; —."[3] And in the beautiful setting of her flower garden, Dickinson observed the hummingbird ride "Upon a single Wheel — / Whose spokes a dizzy Music make" (P 500). Though Dickinson is, indeed, responsive to all of this music of nature, she most specifically hears music in the songs of the birds.

Dickinson's poetry abounds with references to bird songs, and their music provides appropriate imagery for expressing the modulating emotional changes in her life. In one instance a single bird's song could touch her heart, lift her spirits, and encourage her solitary poetic endeavors:

> The Bird her punctual music brings
> And lays it in its place —
> Its place is in the Human Heart
> And in the Heavenly Grace —
> What respite from her thrilling toil
> Did Beauty ever take —
> But Work might be electric Rest
> To those that Magic make — (P 1585)

This is representative of many of Dickinson's bird song poems, for it expresses the dependability of the bird's arrival, the joy its song communicates, and the fact that the "Magic" it makes, like Dickinson's own poetic endeavors, is not "Work" but "electric Rest." In another poem about a solitary bird, "I have a Bird in spring / Which for myself doth sing," Dickinson states that the joy which the robin's song brings to her heart is coupled inevitably with her realization that the cycle of nature requires the bird to depart, although she refuses to "... repine / Knowing that Bird of mine / Though flown — / Learneth beyond the sea / Melody new for me / And will return" (P 5). This poem, written after a disagreement with her sister-in-law Susan and included in a letter to her, shows Dickinson's attempt to reconcile the loss of a beloved object with the hope of eventual reunion. Dickinson interprets the full intent of the poem in a letter to her cousin Louise Norcross: "My birds fly off, nobody knows where they go to, but you see I know they are coming back, and other people don't, that makes the difference" (L 215). In the intervening time, Dickinson expresses to an unnamed loved one that she desires to replace the birds that have flown away, proposing that "Summer for thee, grant I may be / When Summer days are flown! / Thy music still, when Whippoorwill / And Oriole — are done!" (P 31), a poem given the title "Song" when it appeared in *Poems, Third Series* in 1896.

This cycle of nature imagery is seen again in "Before you thought of Spring," a poem which depicts a bird's song as the harbinger of the new season. Here Dickinson describes "A Fellow in the Skies" who brings "specimens of Song / As if for you to choose — / ... And shouts for joy to Nobody / But his seraphic self" (P 1465). Like Dickinson, who often writes poems to please nobody but herself, this bird sings for the sheer pleasure the song brings to itself alone. The music of individual birds is cherished by Dickinson, for, as she wrote to Samuel Bowles in 1861, "the Father's Birds do not all carol at a time — to prove the *cost* of *Music*" (L 242). Dickinson writes of another single bird, who "Unto a silent Sky / Propounded but a single term / Of cautious melody" yet, within an hour, "Her silver Principle / Supplanted all the rest" (P 1084). The bird's initial *pianissimo* notes crescendo to *fortissimo* as the bird's music attains its grand finale, leaving the poet awestruck and with a heart full of song.

In a letter to Dr. and Mrs. Josiah Holland, Dickinson tells of yet another bird whose song has moved her deeply. This letter is particularly noteworthy because it provides distinct clues to Dickinson's poetic aspirations through the metaphor of a bird's song. She writes of finding a small bird that morning, "down — down — on a little bush at the foot of the garden, and wherefore sing, I said, since nobody *hears*? One sob in the throat, one flutter of bosom — 'My business is to *sing*' — and away she rose!" Dickinson suggests to the Hollands that perhaps the song did not go unheard after all, saying, "How do I know but cherubim, once, themselves, as patient, listened, and applauded her unnoticed hymn?" (L 269). Dickinson learns from these birds the long-lasting impact possible from a solitary singer, for to her, "One note from One Bird / Is better than a million words" (Prose Fragment 97), a thought Dickinson expresses in a letter to her friend Helen Hunt Jackson, who was recovering from a broken leg. After promising to watch Jackson's passage "from Crutch to Cane" and from there to "Wings," Dickinson ends her letter with a quatrain about a convalescing bird:

> And then he lifted up his Throat
> And squandered such a Note —
> A Universe that overheard
> Is stricken by it yet — (L 937)

Because of her reputation as a celebrated author, Helen Hunt Jackson's commendation to Dickinson that she was "a great poet" must have had special significance to her, but, in spite of Jackson's admonition that "it is a wrong to the day you live in, that you will not sing aloud" (L 444a), Dickinson continued to believe that publication was "the auction of the mind." The idea of singing appealed to Dickinson, however, and, like the "triumphant Bird" of Poem 1265, she continued to write her poetry for her own " intimate Delight":

> The most triumphant Bird I ever knew or met
> Embarked upon a twig today
> And till Dominion set
> I famish to behold so eminent a sight
> And sang for nothing scrutable
> But intimate Delight.
> Retired, and resumed his transitive Estate —
> To what delicious Accident
> Does finest Glory fit!

Another poem on this same thought describes the pre-dawn singing of the birds which creates "A Music numerous as space — / But neighboring as Noon —," whose "Force" cannot be counted nor witnessed. The music is not given for applause, but for "independent Ecstasy / Of Deity and Men —" (P 783). How perfectly this describes Dickinson's poetry writing, which came as naturally to her as did singing to the birds. The secretive nature of her compositions shows her own "independent Ecstasy / Of Deity and Men —." Though Dickinson's encounters with birds' songs were generally brief, these musical occasions remained in her heart and soul, serving as inspiration for her own artistic endeavors.

Dickinson considered herself a songbird, as she indicates in a letter to her cousin Louise Norcross, and to her sister Vinnie, a houseguest in the Norcross home: "Now, my love, robins, for both of you, and when you and Vinnie sing at sunrise on the apple boughs, just cast your eye to my twig" (L 215). She completes this analogical imagery in Poem 373 by stating her intent to "… perch my Tongue / On Twigs of singing — rather high —." Dickinson's pronounced affinity for birds and the impression their music makes on her "rare ear" is the subject of Poem 760, where the mute plea of a bird "for Charity" evokes such empathy that the poet would give her last crumb, if necessary, to "this Beggar from the Sky." After the bird receives and eats the crumb, it departs and returns "On High" without the least obeisance, a behavior that in a human beggar would be considered discourteous or rude. But then the poet is suddenly surprised when

"Such a Praise began / 'Twas as Space sat singing / To herself — and men —." From this serendipitous experience the poet discerns that "the Winged Beggar" is joyfully "To her Benefactor / Making Gratitude."

Dickinson offers similar thankfulness to Mr. and Mrs. George Montague for their gift of "delightful bread": "I for the first time appreciate the exultation of the robin toward a crumb, though he must be a seductive robin, with whom I would share my own" (L 703). Elsewhere the poet writes, "The Bird must sing to earn the Crumb" (P 880), and in a letter to an aunt, Lucretia Bullard, expressing gratitude for her thoughtfulness, Dickinson includes these lines which were apparently composed for this occasion:

> The Robin for the Crumb
> Returns no syllable
> But long records the Lady's name
> In Silver Chronicle (L 1048).

The seeming neglect of immediate thanks is supplanted eventually by silver melodies of gratitude which are repeated over and over. After her father's death, Dickinson wrote a touching letter to Mrs. Samuel Bowles which provides another instance of deferred gratitude from birds. She relates how her father went to the barn in his slippers one morning for grain to feed cold and frightened birds who had gathered by the kitchen door. Returning from the barn "with a breakfast of grain for each, he hid himself while he scattered it, lest it embarrass them. Ignorant of the name or fate of their benefactor, their descendants are singing this afternoon" (L 644). One wonders if Dickinson knew that highly developed bird songs with a wide range of information are not only inherited but also learned, as this letter about her father's birds implies.

During Dickinson's ebullient moments, the music of the birds uplifts her and creates a spiritual aura around her, as this springtime letter to her friend Jane Humphrey indicates:

> I do wish I could tell you just how the Robins sing — they dont sing now, because it is past their bedtime, and they're all fast asleep, but they *did* sing, this morning, for when we were going

to church, they filled the air with such melody, and sang so deliciously, that I tho't really, Jennie, I never should get to meeting (L 86).

Dickinson often senses God's presence in rapturous encounters such as this and finds she can worship more naturally and reverently in her own garden with God as "a noted Clergyman," ... "a Bobolink for a Chorister" ... and a "little Sexton" who "sings" (P 324).

Though the music of birds could raise Dickinson to heights of ecstasy, it could also plunge her into depths of despair. She finds "A Pang is more conspicuous in Spring / In contrast with the things that sing / " (P 1530), so the singing of birds in the spring could be "The saddest noise, the sweetest noise, / The maddest noise that grows," for it serves as a reminder of the many loved ones from whom death has separated her. At such times, Dickinson finds the birds' songs make her think "... of what we had / And what we now deplore. / We almost wish those siren throats / Would go and sing no more" (P 1764). It is during such depressing times that Dickinson protests, "How dare the robins sing" (P 1724), for their once-joyous melodies have become dissonant strains to her. This despairing thought is expressed in a letter written after the death of her beloved Aunt Lavinia: "The birds keep singing just the same. Oh! The thoughtless birds! ... So many broken-hearted people have got to hear the birds sing ... just the same as if the sun hadn't stopped shining forever!" (L 217). Dickinson wonders, during such periods of mourning, "Why Birds, a Summer morning / Before the Quick of Day / Should stab my ravished spirit / With Dirks of Melody" but rationalizes that such an inquiry will receive the answer only "When Flesh and Spirit sunder" (P 1420). In dolorous instances such as these, bird songs can become the catalyst for producing internal anguish which leads to mental depression.

Perhaps the most poignant expression of nature's indifference to the poet is found in "The Morning after Woe" (P 364), which illustrates the vast chasm that exists between her internal state and the external world. In this poem, the birds, who have so often lifted her spirits and filled her with joy, now

> ... declaim their Tunes —
> Pronouncing every word
> Like Hammers — Did they know they fell
> Like Litanies of Lead —
> On here and there — a creature —
> They'd modify the Glee
> To fit some Crucifixal Clef —
> Some Key of Calvary —

The music of birds profoundly affects Dickinson, and though their songs remain consistent in themselves, the effect of their singing parallels the state of her inner spirit. Once, in a dejected mood, she writes her brother Austin about her great loneliness: "I feel very old every day, and when morning comes and the birds sing, they dont seem to make me so happy as they used to" (L 123).

Several poems about Dickinson's favorite songbird, the ubiquitous robin, illustrate her vacillating emotional stability. In "I dreaded that first Robin, so" (P 348), Dickinson delineates a particular emotional trauma by creating a sense of nightmare. In this poem, Nature, whom she calls "the Gentlest Mother" in Poem 790, is now hostile. To the suffering poet, the robin's song has been transformed into a "Shout" from which, if the poet survives, "Not all Pianos in the Woods /" can "mangle" her. Charles Anderson suggests that "Pianos" is a metaphor for the "treble of the birds, the bass of frogs, and all the range of natural sounds in between, with their wild harmony and counterpoint" in one sense, while in another sense the "Pianos" become "surrealistic instruments of torture."[4] Intense anguish has induced a menacing atmosphere for the poet wherein she is surrounded by inharmonious sounds which are, in reality, merely reflections of her own discordant spirit upon the world of nature. While Dickinson dreads the robin on one hand, on the other she considers that "The Robin's my Criterion for Tune — / Because I grow — where Robins do —" (P 285), a poem exalting the indigenous status that allows her to "see — New Englandly —."

Dickinson combines bird and musical imagery in two famous "companion" poems which deal with epistemological concerns, as a poet and a skeptic theorize on whether true meaning is observable and verifiable or whether it merely resides within the perceiver. One of these poems is "To hear an Oriole sing" (P 526):

> To hear an Oriole sing
> May be a common thing —
> Or only a divine.
>
> It is not of the Bird
> Who sings the same, unheard,
> As unto Crowd —
>
> The Fashion of the Ear
> Attireth that it hear
> In Dun, or fair —
>
> So whether it be Rune,
> Or whether it be none
> Is of within.
>
> The "Tune is in the Tree —"
> The Skeptic — showeth me —
> "No Sir! In Thee!"

The poet proposes that whether the "Rune" is song or mere sound depends on the ear that hears it, since perception alone makes it a 'Tune' and gives it meaning. So when the skeptic asserts that "The Tune is in the Tree —," the poet emphatically replies, "No Sir! In Thee!"

Dickinson again raises questions about the origin of song in a kindred poem, "Split the Lark — and you'll find the Music" (P 861):

> Split the Lark — and you'll find the Music —
> Bulb after Bulb, in Silver rolled —
> Scantily dealt to the Summer Morning
> Saved for your Ear when Lutes be old.
>
> Loose the Flood — you shall find it patent —
> Gush after Gush, reserved for you —
> Scarlet Experiment! Sceptic Thomas!
> Now, do you doubt that your Bird was true?

Once again, the skeptic seeks verifiable proof of the source of the lark's song, but his desire to "Split the Lark" in order to "find the Music" would be futile since the "Silver" songs are rolled up in "Bulb after Bulb" of the *living* lark, whose nature it is to sing and whose life is reflected in song. Because Dickinson often presents her imaginary self as a bird, as one whose "business" it is "to sing," this poem about the song within the bird becomes analogous to the vision of the poem within the poet.

Bird song is a classic image for unfettered lyric expression. Dickinson's own equation of the bird with the poet, and of its music with poetry, was first revealed in the mid-eighteen-fifties, when she had gained confidence in her talent, prompting her to move from novice to artist. In two letters of this period, Dickinson alludes to this change in language that characteristically combines disguise with disclosure concerning her new vocation. In a letter to her uncle, Joseph Sweetser, Dickinson tells of the transformation through which she has gone:

> Much has occurred, dear Uncle, since my writing you — so much — that I stagger as I write, in its sharp remembrance. Summer of bloom — and months of frost, and days of jingling bells, … There is a smiling summer here, which causes birds to sing, and sets the bees in motion…. I would you saw what I can see, and imbibed this music. The day went down, long time ago, and still a simple choir bear the canto on … I hardly know what I have said — my words put all their feathers on — and fluttered here and there (L 190).

And to Louise Norcross, Dickinson hints at the poetic future she began to envision for herself when she recalls the time the two of them "decided to be distinguished": "It's a great thing to be 'great,' Loo, and you and I might tug for a life, and never accomplish it, but no one can stop our looking on, and you know some cannot sing, but the orchard is full of birds, and we all can listen. What if we learn, ourselves, someday! Who indeed knows?" (L 199). Years later, around 1880, Dickinson wrote to Mrs. Elizabeth Carmichael, "I am studying music now with the jays, and find them charming artists" (L 665), indicating the ongoing musical development of her girlhood vision.

Dickinson's present status as one of the world's great lyric poets provides evidence that she did indeed learn to "sing." The elaboration of her "singing" talent, however, came at great cost. In "Why — do they shut Me out of Heaven?" she asks, "Did I sing — too loud?" (P 248). She does not understand why she is deprived of heaven but senses it has something to do with writing poetry which is too daring, presumptuous, and innovative for a woman of her time. Self-indulgence, no matter how harmless, was a sin in Emily Dickinson's Puritan world, and writing poetry for one's own artistic release would constitute self-indulgence carried to its heights in a society where even letter writing on the Sabbath Day was banned. Dickinson's early recognition of her poetic talent may well have had much to do with her inability to give herself up totally to the claims of Christ when so many of her friends and members of her family "flocked to the ark of safety" during the Great Revival of 1850. Dickinson's dilemma at this time is revealed in a letter to her friend Jane Humphrey, for in it Dickinson professes that "the path of duty looks ugly indeed, and the place where *I* want to go more amiable — a great deal." In this same letter, Dickinson confesses that it is so much easier "to do wrong than right — so much pleasanter to be evil than good, I dont wonder that good angels weep — and bad ones sing songs" (L 30). Dickinson struggled with this dichotomy throughout her life, and in this poem of rejection she expresses her desire to win heavenly acceptance and divine favor by adopting a more suitable stance when she suggests, "But — I can say a little 'Minor' / Timid as a Bird!" (P 248).

Dickinson's longing for future recognition and her continued application of the song analogy to herself as poet are revealed in this letter to her sister-in-law Susan: "Could I make you and Austin — proud — sometime — a great way off — 'twould give me taller feet —" (L 238). Particularly significant in conjunction with this note is its poetic counterpoint:

> I shall keep singing!
> Birds will pass me
> On their way to Yellower Climes
> Each — with a Robin's expectation —
> I — with my Redbreast —
> And my Rhymes —
>
> Late — when I take my place in summer —
> But — I shall bring a fuller tune —
> Vespers — are sweeter than Matins — Signor —
> Morning — only the seed of Noon — (P 250)

Here Dickinson reveals her belief that future acknowledgment of her poetry will be more meaningful than early acceptance would have been. She prophetically projects that it will be "Late" — when she takes her "place in summer —," "But," she adds with confidence, "I shall bring a fuller tune —." She is content to express symbolically that "Vespers," those songs sung late in the day, "are sweeter than Matins —," those songs sung in the morning. Dickinson's desire for future recognition and for the fulfillment of her poetic powers, if only by herself and for herself, keeps a song in her heart and is the subject of Poem 254: "'Hope' is the thing with feathers — / That perches in the soul — / And sings the tune without the words — / And never stops — at all — /." The poem continues to deduce the bird's song "... sweetest — in the Gale — is heard — / ," a prevalent theme in the bird song poems, that of singing through adversity and pain. Without hope there is no endurance, Dickinson believed, prompting her to praise a bird she knew "that would sing as firm in the centre of Dissolution, as in it's Father's nest —" (L 685).

"Not with a Club, the Heart is broken / Nor with a Stone" (P 1304) makes a memorable song out of suffering as one of the pressures which extricates poetry from the heart. Here, a boy kills the bird of his desire, heedless of its song, yet the "Magnanimous" bird sings "... unto the Stone / Of which it died —." This stoic quality is mentioned in one of Dickinson's letters to her "Master": "If you saw a bullet hit a Bird — and he told you he was'nt shot — you might weep at his courtesy, but you would certainly doubt his word" (L 233). She develops this idea poetically in "Her smile was shaped like other smiles —" in which a woman's internal anguish is masked by her external appearance. Her seemingly ordinary smile is compared to a bird who "Did hoist herself, to sing, / Then recollect a Ball, she got — / And hold upon the Twig, / Convulsive, while the Music broke — / Like Beads — among the Bog —" (P 514). Once again, a lone bird sings through its pain with no audience to hear, a description which aptly suits Dickinson's poetic endeavors.

In another "Master" directed plea, Dickinson writes, "One drop more from the gash that stains your Daisy's bosom — then would you *believe*?" (L 233). Dickinson converts the thought of this prose statement into a poem which indicates that she may have been familiar with an old English legend about the robin. According to the legend, this "pious bird with the scarlet breast" mercifully picked a thorn from the crown of Christ as He was on His way to Calvary. As the bird carried the thorn in its beak, a drop of blood fell from the thorn to its breast, dyeing it red. Through musical terminology, Dickinson transforms this legend into a ballad:

> Sang from the Heart, Sire,
> Dipped my Beak in it,
> If the Tune drip too much
> Have a tint too Red
>
> Pardon the Cochineal —
> Suffer the Vermilion —
> Death is the Wealth
> Of the Poorest Bird.
>
> Bear with the Ballad —
> Awkward — faltering —
> Death twists the strings —
> 'Twasn't my blame —
>
> Pause in your Liturgies —
> Wait your Chorals —
> While I repeat your
> Hallowed name — (P 1059)

Here the bird song and the heart song are one, depicting a passionate devotion which endures until death.

Dickinson finds that bird song provides appropriate imagery for expressing both her pleasure and her pain, but she often uses her own voice in solo song to reveal equally deep emotions. In a sympathetic letter written to her Norcross cousins on the death of their father, Dickinson asks them to "Let Emily sing for you because she cannot pray" (L 278). In another letter to these cousins, she expresses astonishment that Robert Browning had written another poem following the death of his wife — "till I remembered that I, myself, in my smaller way, sang off charnel steps" (L 298).

For Dickinson, "singing" is as necessary as breathing and no amount of constriction can prevent her from doing so. In one poem, she declares, "Bind me — I still can sing — / Banish — my mandolin / Strikes true within — / Slay — and my Soul shall rise / Chanting to Paradise — / Still thine." (P 1005). In her second letter to Higginson, Dickinson explains one of the reasons for her singing: "I had a terror — since September — I could tell to none — and so I sing, as the Boy does by the Burying Ground — because I am afraid" (L 261). These words, which have often been used to explain why Dickinson turned to poetry for emotional release, provide some basis for the idea that her obsession with the theme of extreme pain had its origin in a traumatic personal experience of unusual magnitude.

Dickinson related this extreme suffering to separation from a loved one in a poem written in 1864, which begins and ends with phraseology remarkably similar to her statement to Higginson. In Poem 850, singing becomes a coping strategy to allay the pangs of separation from a loved one:

> I sing to use the Waiting
> My Bonnet but to tie
> And shut the Door unto my House
> No more to do have I
>
> Till His best step approaching
> We journey to the Day
> And tell each other how We sung
> To Keep the Dark away.

Here singing becomes the means by which the speaker can function through daily life and can endure the intervening time until the two lovers are united, presumably in heaven. The speaker can be ready for the journey with her loved one in a moment's notice, at which time they will share with each other "how We sung / To Keep the Dark away."

In a number of poems, Dickinson uses music itself as a metaphor for describing the effect of scintillating experiences and of divine illuminations. In reporting "earthly intimations of immortality," Eberwein rightly observes that Dickinson most often relied upon the language of music — "most ethereal of the arts, most abstractly harmonious, and most traditionally associated with images of heaven."[5] Poem 503 serves as an extraordinary example of Dickinson's ability to convey "earthly intimations of immortality" through the language of music. Here she must delineate her exhilarating experience through contrasts, however, since no adequate comparisons exist to relate the supernatural epiphany which came to her alone:

> Better — than Music! For I — who heard it —
> I was used — to the Birds — before —
> This — was different — 'Twas Translation —
> Of all tunes I knew — and more —
>
> 'Twasn't contained — like other stanza —
> No one could play it — the second time —
> But the Composer — perfect Mozart —
> Perish with him — that Keyless Rhyme!
>
> . . . .
>
> Not such a strain — the Church — baptizes —
> When the last Saint — goes up the Aisles —
> Not such a stanza splits the silence —
> When the Redemption strikes her Bells —
>
> Let me not spill — its smallest cadence —
> Humming — for promise — when alone —
> Humming — until my faint Rehearsal —
> Drop into tune — around the Throne —

Here the poet hears incomparable, once-in-a-lifetime music, in "Keyless Rhyme" unrestrained by form or stanza. So exalted is she by this experience that she believes no better melody could ever have existed, even in Eden before the "Fall." She tells of a tune she has heard herself, not one she has heard about, and she recognizes that ritualistic theology would not sanction her personal revelation, so she can only hum in "faint Rehearsal" until she can "Drop into tune — around the Throne —." This musical ode all but sings itself in joyous recital, and the occasion it recounts sparks Dickinson's intuition that "This World is not Conclusion." Whatever stands beyond is "Invisible, as Music — / But positive, as Sound —" (P 501). Here, as in "Better than Music!", she demonstrates her fascination with immortality while simultaneously rejecting currently accepted religious dogma.

Dickinson continues her attempt to speculate on intimations of immortality in "The Love a Life can show Below" (P 673), a poem contrasting human and divine love which relies on the language of music:

> The Love a Life can show Below
> Is but a filament, I know,
> Of that diviner thing
> That faints upon the face of Noon —
> And smites the Tinder in the Sun —
> And hinders Gabriel's Wing —
>
> 'Tis this — in Music — hints and sways —
> And far abroad on Summer days —
> Distils uncertain pain —
> 'Tis this enamors in the East —
> And tints the Transit in the West
> With harrowing Iodine —
>
> 'Tis this —invites — appalls — endows —
> Flits — glimmers — proves — dissolves —
> Returns — suggests — convicts — enchants —
> Then — flings in Paradise —

Though the poet affirms the vastly superior glory of divine love, she can only describe it in terms taken from "Below." For Dickinson, music is instrumental in expressing that which is beyond human cognition by its effect on the perceiver.

In Poem 1480, Dickinson again struggles valiantly against human limitations in an attempt to express the ineffable:

> The fascinating chill that music leaves
> Is Earth's corroboration
> Of Ecstasy's impediment —
> 'Tis Rapture's germination
> In timid and tumultuous soil
> A fine — estranging creature —
> To something upper wooing us
> But not to our Creator —

Music here becomes the means by which one is transported into a realm of emotional exaltation beyond earthly bounds. In all of these poems whose theme is immortality, music is Dickinson's chosen metaphor for describing the multiple aspects of heavenly love and of heavenly visions not explainable in human terms.

Possibly Dickinson's deepest, most questing look at immortality through musical terms is found in her letter to Charles H. Clark in mid-October of 1883: "Dear friend, These thoughts disquiet me, and the great friend is gone, who could solace them. Do they disturb you?" (L 872). Dickinson expresses her emotional quandary in poetic form in what would become Poem 1576 and includes it in this letter. Here music plays a major role in her speculation on the eternal question of man's existence after death, a question as old as recorded history. In ancient biblical literature, Job posed the question, "If a man dies, will he live again?" (Job 14:14), and Dickinson echoes this inquiry when she asserts and then questions that "The Spirit lasts — but in what mode —." She recognizes that on earth "the Body speaks, / But as the Spirit furnishes — / Apart, it never talks —," prompting this perceptive musical analogy:

> The Music in the Violin
> Does not emerge alone
> But Arm in Arm with Touch, yet Touch
> Alone — is not a Tune —

The question of how the soul can manifest itself without the body remains unanswered, but her musical descriptions bring tangible substance to complex, intangible thoughts about immortality. Six years before her death in 1886, Dickinson expresses her continuing perplexity on this subject in a letter to Maria Whitney: "I am constantly more astonished that the Body contains the Spirit — Except for overmastering work it could not be borne" (L 643).

Music, despite all its often exhilarating qualities, could also create the atmosphere for depths of emotional despair. One of Dickinson's finest poems on despair is "There's a certain Slant of light" (P 258), wherein a certain condition of nature induces a feeling of painful oppressiveness in the poet. Here, a "Heavenly Hurt" is analogous to the "Heft of Cathedral Tunes," weighty, solemn, and majestic like organ music. Music comes nearest to describing this mood of longing and sadness in the poet's heart which occurs on "Winter Afternoons —," for, as Dickinson expressed in a letter to Higginson, "These

Behaviors of the Year hurt almost like Music — shifting when it ease us most" (L 381).

Poem 315 describes an even greater experience of "Heavenly Hurt" in which the personality is all but irreparably shattered:

> He fumbles at your Soul
> As Players at the Keys
> Before they drop full Music on —
> He stuns you by degrees —
> Prepares your brittle Nature
> For the Ethereal Blow
> By fainter Hammers — further heard —
> Then nearer — Then so slow
> Your Breath has time to straighten —
> Your Brain — to bubble Cool —
> Deals — One — imperial — Thunderbolt —
> That scalps your naked Soul —
>
> When Winds take Forests in their Paws —
> The Universe — is still —

With unusual emotional intensity which builds to a climax, Dickinson describes the gradual process through which a soul may undergo manipulation from an outside force. With this force, or master-figure as pianist and the self as the pounded piano, Dickinson once again employs musical imagery to suggest the dynamic impact, and even the anguish, of divine intervention as an essential part of the human experience.

According to Adrienne Rich, "Dickinson is *the* American poet whose work consisted in exploring states of psychic extremity."[6] John Cody, in his psychoanalytical study of Emily Dickinson's life, claims that she possessed "a greater capacity for the perception and discrimination of psychological processes and a greater ability to find appropriate words to express her inner experiences than any patient who has ever been psychoanalyzed."[7] Very often, those "appropriate words" are expressed in musical terminology, as evidenced in two of Dickinson's most famous poems of this type, where music becomes the mode which helps to express her internal conflict and to face her genuine fears of psychic dissolution without total loss of control. In "The first

Day's Night had come" (P 410), the poet has a dialogue with her "Soul" — that is, her inner psychic self, her ego:

> The first Day's Night had come —
> And grateful that a thing
> So terrible — had been endured —
> I told my Soul to sing —
>
> She said her Strings were snapt —
> Her Bow — to Atoms blown —
> And so to mend her — gave me work
> Until another Morn —
>
> And then — a Day as huge
> As Yesterdays in pairs,
> Unrolled its horror in my face —
> Until it blocked my eyes —
>
> My Brain — begun to laugh —
> I mumbled — like a fool —
> And tho' 'tis Years ago — that Day —
> My Brain keeps giggling — still.
>
> And Something's odd — within —
> That person that I was —
> And this One — do not feel the same —
> Could it be Madness — this?

When she tells her soul to sing, which for Dickinson means to celebrate her poetic gift by releasing her feelings in poetry, her soul cannot comply because "her Strings were snapt — / Her Bow — to Atoms blown — / ." Here Dickinson shows her knowledge of the doctrine of the harmony of the soul as espoused by many of the ancient Greek philosophers, who compared the soul to a stringed instrument, notably a lyre. For them, emotional and spiritual balance were reflections of well-tuned strings in the instrument of the soul. In this poem, Dickinson recognizes that the tension of the strings of her soul are not properly adjusted and have been strained to excessive heights through some unnamed anguish until they have "snapt," leaving her mentally and spiritually bereft. When her soul is unable to sing, she resorts to laughing, mumbling and giggling "like a fool," prompting the poet to ask, "Could it be Madness — this?"

Another description of the fractured soul is found in "The Soul has Bandaged moments" (P 512), particularly in verses one, three and five:

> The Soul has Bandaged moments —
> When too appalled to stir —
> She feels some ghastly Fright come up
> And stop to look at her —
>
> . . . .
>
> The soul has moments of Escape —
> When bursting all the doors —
> She dances like a Bomb, abroad,
> And swings upon the Hours,
>
> . . . .
>
> The Soul's retaken moments —
> When, Felon led along,
> With shackles on the plumed feet,
> And staples, in the Song,

Through moments of madness, the imprisoned soul escapes its bondage, transcends all limitations and "dances like a Bomb, abroad." The temporary freedom and the exhilaration it brings are bittersweet, however, for these radical variations between confinement and liberty create a condition more limiting than before. The "retaken" Soul now recognizes its lost freedom and power, its dancing "plumed feet" now wear "shackles" and its triumphant "Song" is now punctured with "staples." Musical imagery once again conveys a recurring theme in Dickinson's poetry, that ecstasy does not last, but that it is given and then removed, leaving the victim with a renewed sense of destitution.

A similar feeling of deprivation is evident in "I've dropped my Brain — My Soul is numb — " wherein the speaker's once-vital life, with its "Instincts for Dance," has become "Carved and cool," and her once-paradisiacal life has become stone-like and turned to marble, causing her to wonder, "Who wrought Carrara in me / And chiselled all my tune" (P 1046). Once again, Dickinson expresses that losing the tune, the music of her poetry, would be to lose her desire to exist. She addresses this theme again in "As from the earth the light Balloon / Asks nothing but release — ," a poem representing the release of the spirit from the body. Here, "The spirit looks upon the Dust / That fastened it so long / With indignation, / As a Bird / Defrauded of its song" (P 1630). Dickinson's passion to express her innermost thoughts through her musical poetry constituted the basis of her life. In a somewhat theatrical and whimsical account of what her own ascension into immortality might be like, she indicates that she will be writing her "music" until the very end of her life:

> Dying at my music!
> Bubble! Bubble!
> Hold me till the Octave's run!
> Quick! Burst the Windows!
> Ritardando!
> Phials left, and the Sun! (P 1003)

The music becomes gradually slower and finally ceases as the process of dying accelerates. Here Dickinson enacts the thoughts she shared with John Graves in 1856 when she wrote to him about the quick flight of time and the things which have already changed and passed away. She wrote, "We, too, are flying — fading, John — and the song 'here lies,' soon upon lips that love us now — will have hummed and ended" (L 184). Immortality and music were bound together in Dickinson's mind, as she so often indicates in her poems and her letters. Music somehow "fit" her for the world to come, as she professes in a letter to Mrs. Howard Sweetser two years before she died. The Sweetser's son Howard had come to the Homestead to sing for Dickinson, and her letter reveals that she had "felt some uncertainty as to my qualification for the final Redemption, but the delightful Melody has entirely fitted me —" (L 920). That music transported Dickinson from the corporeal world to the spiritual one is evident throughout her works.

Though numerous other poems and letters contain musical imagery, these varied examples show that music is the nexus that Dickinson employs to join such disparate subjects as human relationships, nature, immortality, and emotional pain and suffering. Clearly, musical imagery lends strength, beauty, and meaning to Dickinson's poems and letters. Yet literary reviews from the last decade of the nineteenth century indicate that early reviewers and critics were not so enamored of the musical imagery of Dickinson's verse as they were with the over-all musical quality of it. Inspection of some of these reviews in the following chapter reveals some remarkably sensitive responses to the musicality of Dickinson's poems and letters.

CHAPTER III

Musical Qualities
of Dickinson's Poetry:
Nineteenth-Century Views

The discovery of Emily Dickinson's poems shortly after her death in 1886 remains one of the major events in American literary history. When her sister Lavinia found almost eighteen hundred poems in Emily's dresser drawers, she realized that she had discovered a veritable treasure, but she could never have dreamed of the world-wide and enduring ramifications of her incredible find. Her immediate desire was to have them published in a limited number of copies to share with special friends, and the urgency with which she pursued this project was perhaps generated from the fact that she had already destroyed numerous manuscripts and letters which had been sent to Emily, many of them from nationally recognized people. Lavinia's appeals for help with the publication of the poems began with her sister-in-law Susan Dickinson, with whom Emily had shared many lofty thoughts and poetic aspirations. Susan's literary influence on Emily had been extensive, as Emily's letter of 1882 to Susan reveals: "With the exception of Shakespeare, you have told me of more knowledge than any one living —" (L 757). Susan's early enthusiasm for the project turned to indifference and finally to discouragement of publication at all. Lavinia then approached Thomas Wentworth Higginson, prominent man of letters and the "Preceptor" from whom Emily Dickinson sought literary advice over a period of twenty years, sending him 102 poems enclosed in seventy-one letters. Higginson, who had admired Emily's dazzling thoughts while deploring her lack of form, declined Lavinia's offer, protesting that his busy schedule and the near-cryptic status of the poems presented insuperable obstacles for his participation in such an undertaking. He did, however, agree to go over the poems if they could be put into careful shape for consideration. Lavinia's last alternative, Mabel Loomis Todd, a friend of the family who had artistic gifts in the fields of art, music, and literature, proved to be her best choice, for Todd was "technically the best equipped person in town to edit the poems,"[1] and the importance of her acceptance of the formidable tasks of transcribing Dickinson's poems and of finding publishers for them cannot be overstated. Without Todd's vision, her tenacity, her intuitive insight into Dickinson's genius, and, perhaps most importantly, her *faith* in the poems, there is a distinct possibility that Dickinson's creative efforts might have been lost to the literary world completely.

Instead, Todd devoted much of the next ten years of her life to preparing the poems for publication, to acting as co-editor with Thomas Wentworth Higginson of the first two series of *Poems by Emily Dickinson*, and to becoming sole editor of the third series and of the two-volume *Letters of Emily Dickinson*. Also, Todd made a significant contribution to the study of nineteenth-century literary criticism by collecting and preserving hundreds of original magazine and newspaper reviews about Dickinson's poems and letters in separate scrapbooks for each of the three volumes of poems and a single scrapbook for the two-volume edition of letters. She obviously comprehended the importance of saving these documents for posterity because she took the same thoughtful care in compiling these clippings as she had taken in editing the poems and the letters. She saved brief notices as well as lengthy ones, and she hired a professional service to obtain all known comments and reviews from areas beyond her purview.

In 1989, Willis J. Buckingham almost doubled Mabel Todd's collection of 325 reviews when he edited his *Emily Dickinson's Reception in the 1890s: A Documentary History,* yet he acknowledges that it is "to

Todd's vision and effort that credit for his book's comprehensiveness must largely fall."[2] The six hundred entries in Buckingham's volume include all known commentary on Dickinson published in the eighteen-nineties, thus providing a rare and exceptionally broad perspective for assessing American verse criticism and book publishing during the last decade of the nineteenth century. Because these primary sources have been virtually unavailable until the publication of Buckingham's book, the tendency has been toward generalization of information rather than specific focus on specialized topics. Therefore, Buckingham says, "the fullest promise of these reviews will finally lie in the capacity of new generations of readers to discover in them—and to compose out of them—yet another valued constituent of their own patient questioning of Dickinson's words."[3] In the light of that promise, these reviews have been scrutinized for what they might yield to this study of Emily Dickinson and music, and the search has provided surprising and deeply satisfying results.

The diverse reactions found in the nineteenth-century reviews prompts contemporary scholars to ask two major questions: "Why was Emily Dickinson liked so well?" and "Why was she liked so little?"[4] Out of a number of potential answers to these questions, two distinct possibilities prevail consistently throughout the criticism. First, Dickinson was "liked so well" because of the musical qualities of her verse, and, second, she was "liked so little" because of the seeming lack of form in her poetry. Examination of some key nineteenth-century reviews illustrates these reactions and provides insight into the acceptance and the rejection of Dickinson's verse by her contemporary, or near-contemporary, readers and reviewers.

Many of the earliest literary critics and reviewers recognized the musical quality of Dickinson's verse, and nineteenth-century criticism is replete with analogies connecting Emily Dickinson and music. Dickinson often compared herself to a bird and her poetry to song, and critics of the last decade of the nineteenth century appear to have agreed with that analogy. One critic wrote of Dickinson's poetry, "Surely there were never such 'wood-notes' warbled in lovelier and more silvery trebles,"[5] and another, writing for *Truth*, the New York weekly of high society and social satire, called Dickinson "the strangely gifted, recluse singer," finding that she has "a native impulse to harmony often attaining the melody akin to a wild-bird's song."[6] One article in the "Books and Authors" section of the *Boston Sunday Courier* addresses Dickinson's great intellectual activity and its incomparable results, the accomplishment of verse, in these terms:

> As a caged thrush sings, so sang she, for the sake of singing and
> of making beautiful her place in the world, while she might....
> It is true, we liken this singer to the thrush in the cage, because
> of the calm environment with which she chose to surround her
> movements. It is equally true that her song is as untutored, as
> wild, free and lovely as the thrush's song, with clear, sure notes,
> bearing messages ever.[7]

A similar thought, written for the *Boston Daily Traveller,* supports the "freedom and fullness" of Dickinson's verse as "the expression of the inward thought," without concern for either criticism or praise, claiming that it "has a charm as indefinable as the song of a wild bird that sings out of the fullness of its heart. There is no fear of discord."[8] And, in the first discussion of Emily Dickinson in a language other than English, the German critic "A. Von E." wrote an appreciative essay comparing Dickinson to a German woman poet, Annette von Droste-Hulshoff. Acknowledging their differences in regard to publication, the article states that the German poet thought of publishing her poems as early as her youth, while "the American poet, bird-like, sang spontaneously for herself alone."[9] Rupert Hughes, speaking of the startling originality and the captivating individuality of Dickinson's ideas in an 1896 article for *Godey's Magazine,* placed her above all other female poets. Though recognizing that Dickinson is a grievous sinner against rhyme and metre, he finds "such a rush and fire to her measures" that he likens it to "the gushing outburst of an improvisatory bird, careless of Richterian theories of eight measures to the period, careless of everything but of voicing itself just as it feels."[10]

The vast majority of comparisons between Dickinson's verse and bird song were positive ones, but Dickinson's severest critic, the Englishman Andrew Lang, took every occasion to make negative comments on this American poet whom he could not understand. In one column for *Illustrated London News*, Lang wrote that "one might as well seek for an air in the notes of a bird as for articulate and sustained poetry here."[11] In another, he attacked William Dean Howells for the article he wrote for *Harper's New Monthly Magazine* in praise of Dickinson's poem, "New feet within my garden go." In his review, Howells wrote such accolades as "there is a still, solemn, rapt movement of the thought and music together that is of exquisite charm" and "This is a song that sings itself."[12] Lang, who failed to catch the music of the poem which Howells so clearly heard, retaliates with the following observations on the same poem: "What in the world has a troubadour to do in New England? And why did he climb a tree? Or was he a bird? And how can solitude be betrayed by a troubadour, somewhere near Boston, in the foliage of an elm?" In fact, Lang fails to find anything of value in the poem at all, saying, "There are no words that can say how bad poetry may be when it is divorced from meaning, from music, from grammar, from rhyme; in brief, from articulate and intelligible speech."[13] Though Lang's evaluation seems almost an embarrassment to present-day critics of Dickinson's poetry, it is nevertheless important because of the light it sheds on the varying attitudes regarding the musical qualities of Dickinson's poetry during the nineteenth century.

The majority of critics and readers who commented on music in their articles found it to be one of the most attractive qualities of Dickinson's verse. Many of the reviewers praised Dickinson and her poems through the medium of musical terminology. Possibly the most extravagant example of applying musical terms to describe Dickinson and her poetry is in this article which Samuel J. Barrows wrote for the *Christian Register*:

> Miss Dickinson was a recluse. She communed very little with society, but much with nature and with her own mind. She was not made to play a part in the world's great orchestra. She was more like an Aeolian harp through which the wind swept over a delicately attuned nature, sometimes awaking the minor, sometimes the major chord, and now and then striking a dissonant note which only seemed to give more richness and piquancy to the harmony. Her poetry was never made of sustained notes or flowing strains. It was made of little gusts of song, snatches of melody, broken chords, and arpeggios.[14]

Though not all the reviews used musical terminology so pro-
fusely, a great many of them found that music provided an extremely
appropriate figurative language by which Dickinson and her poetry
could be described. One anonymous reviewer, writing for the *Fall
River* [Massachusetts] *Monitor*, commented on the large sale of the
second series of Emily Dickinson's poems and on the most cordial
commendation from press reviews of the poems, in spite of the fact
that Dickinson was a comparatively unknown writer. This reviewer
found that "her verses are not merely those bits of exquisite melody
that catch the fancy and haunt the memory with their sweetness.
Melodious as is much of Miss Dickinson's versification, it is not the
chief or the most marked characteristic of her writing," which the
author believed to be her deep thought and strong originality.[15] Robert
Bridges, in an article for *Life*, one of the most elegant and cultivated
magazines in America during the eighteen-nineties, asserted that those
who like philosophy in verse will easily find it in Dickinson's poetry,
but he suggests that they will probably overlook what is a finer thing—
"the original fancy which compresses striking images into a few words,
or catches a strange melody in most irregular measures."[16]

One reviewer of "Books and Bookmen" in *Light*, the society and
entertainment weekly for Worcester, Massachusetts, commented on
the incredible interest and admiration that the first series of Dickinson's poems evoked and mentions that the preface in the second series
acquaints the readers, to a limited extent, with the writer herself. It
reveals "what a remarkable being she was, unquestionably, divinely
touched by the spirit of song."[17] An article in the *Boston Home Journal* section, "Books and Authors," praises the first volume of *Poems by
Emily Dickinson*, predicting that it will become a cherished companion to thousands of lovers of poetry who never even heard of Emily
Dickinson's name, but who will at once recognize "the richness of the
mind of her who was wont to sing from a heart overflowing with love
for nature and humanity."[18] Another musical comment on this first
book of poems, found in the "New Books" section of the Boston independent review and opinion weekly *Commonwealth*, states that Dickinson had no wish for publicity, no desire for fame, and "no ambition
to sing in accord with other poets."[19] In a review for the *Springfield
Republican* addressing Dickinson's unique style, Charles Goodrich

Whiting avers that literary form, as used by others, she regarded little. Instead, she was determined to express herself just as she did, "having her own standard of rhythm, or perhaps we should say music, and her own choice of words."[20]

Thomas Wentworth Higginson himself, Dickinson's preceptor and a highly respected literary critic, in a review for "Recent Poetry" in *Nation*, possibly the country's leading weekly periodical commenting on politics and letters, promoted Dickinson's work in these musical terms:

> Emily Dickinson resolutely refused to publish her verses, showing them only to a very few friends. As a consequence, she had almost no criticism, and was absolutely untrammelled; so that the verses are sometimes almost formless, while at other times they show great capacity for delicate and sweet melody, suggesting the chance strains of an Aeolian harp. But in compass of thought, grasp of feeling, and vigor of epithet, they are simply extraordinary, and strike notes, very often, like those of some deep-toned organ."[21]

Poet and critic Bliss Carmen, in a review for the *Chicago Post*, made a similar observation when he claimed that "Emily Dickinson's peculiar scheme of rhyme was handled with such mastery, with such an exquisite ear for cadence, as to become in her hands a new and original stop in the great organ of English versification."[22]

Edward J. Harding began his review in "Today's Literature" for the *Chicago Tribune* in 1891 by quoting Dickinson's "And the noise in the pool at noon excels my piano," lines she once sent to Thomas Wentworth Higginson. Harding, literary editor for the *Tribune*, perceived that Dickinson was "groping after a music more spiritual than is made on the piano." This was a mood he claimed to be seeking for himself "in the shadowy recesses of his inner consciousness," which, he claimed, "gives a premonitory quiver when it encounters a rhythmical nature such as Emily Dickinson, who had a delicacy of expression like Chopin's—she was a New England Chopin—a Chopin living in the bleak-soul-unfavorable conditions of the Yankee atmosphere."[23] This somewhat startling comparison is nonetheless appropriate, for Chopin's great appreciation for the effects the piano could produce matched Dickinson's respect for the effects induced by poetry, and his finest works, like those of Dickinson's, were in forms that he himself worked out or perfected. The astounding musicality of Dickinson's verse coupled with the American quality of the New England land-scape and atmosphere make Harding's analogy of these two artists both pertinent and viable.

The instant popularity of the first series of Emily Dickinson's poetry and of the two series which followed "is something unique in literature, being wholly posthumous and achieved without puffing or special effort, and indeed, quite contrary to the expectation of both editors and publishers," according to Higginson in his 1896 review for "Recent Poetry" in *Nation*. He added the following comment, which can only be viewed as extraordinary in light of his early and persis-tent discouragement to Emily Dickinson herself about publication: "No volumes of American poetry, not even the most popular of Longfellow's, have had so wide or so steady a sale."[24]

Mabel Loomis Todd, in her comments on public reaction to Dickinson's poetry, claimed that the critics hardly knew where to place Emily Dickinson's "strangely compelling poems" when they were first published. Todd, by reading and comparing the many notices about Dickinson's poetry, found that the reviewers agreed in allowing her the possession of undoubted genius, while at the same time they deplored the fact that Dickinson seemed to care so slightly for the form in which her "startling little poetic bombs were cast."[25] In an 1895 "tea talk" in Worcester, Massachusetts, Todd acknowledged the general agreement of critics about Dickinson's lack of form, but she expressed her deeper understanding of Dickinson's poems by saying, "Yet there is a strange cadence of hidden music underlying her verse, which is like an orchid growing among the ordinary flowers of the field."[26] A writer for "Poems Fresh From the Press" in the *Cleveland Sunday Plain Dealer* picked up on Todd's observation that Dickinson's verses all show a strange cadence of inner rhythmical music, adding that, "Charmed by that music and seized by the thought the reader does not discover until upon closer investigation that her lines are dar-ingly constructed and frequently defy all accepted rules of versifica-tion."[27]

The controversy between form and substance in Dickinson's

poetry was a consistent one during the last decade of the nineteenth century, with critics somewhat divided in their attitudes. Many of them, accustomed to the conventional poetic patterns of the day, found Dickinson's departure from accepted forms highly distasteful, while others applauded her rare ability to achieve a sense of rhythm while disregarding the form of it. And, surprisingly, quite a number of critics combined these attitudes, acknowledging that their blending demonstrated Dickinson's capacity to achieve poetic thought in her own, quite original way. Critics in the last two groups almost invariably recognized the musicality of Dickinson's verse as the ingredient which most clearly qualified her works as poetry.

Arlo Bates, well known in the New England area as a poet, novelist, critic, and literary editor, provided an example of the combined attitude toward Dickinson's poetry in his "Books and Authors" review for the *Boston Sunday Courier* in 1890. In the first place, he found that "there is hardly a line in the entire volume, and certainly not a stanza, which cannot be objected to upon the score of technical imperfection," and he claimed that Dickinson was "as unlearned in the technical side of art as if she had written when the forms of verse had not yet been invented.... Her ear had certainly not been susceptible of training to the appreciation of form and melody, or it is inconceivable that she should have written as she did." Having said that, Bates nonetheless acknowledged that there is hardly a line of her work "which fails to throw out some gleam of genuine original power, of imagination, and of real emotional thought," and he declared that it was "the muse herself and no other who inspired Miss Dickinson's songs."[28] A year later, Mary D. Cutting acknowledged in her review for "Literature" in the *Christian Inquirer* that the charge to be brought against Dickinson's poems is their lack of rhyme and their want of finished form, yet she contended that they are not wanting in metrical movement. That, she claimed, is usually original and sustained, so that, "borne along by the poetic thought and musical movement, the absence of rhymes is at times almost lost sight of." Cutting believed that Dickinson's poems do not always violate poetical techniques, and occasionally there appears "a strain of musical rhythm and flow, suggesting the conclusion that its common absence is from choice or perhaps the necessity to sing after unconventional methods. She is not lyric; she will not charm the fancy by the cadence of her verse, but she will stir the heart by its melodic note."[29]

One writer for the *Concord People and Patriot* found that Dickinson excluded everything that could interfere with her thought, generally sacrificing rhyme and rhetoric, However, this writer conceded that "whatever Dickinson's lines may neglect in form, they accord with the inner soul of harmony."[30] An anonymous critic writing on Dickinson's poems for *Housekeeper's Weekly* in 1892 found her verses so running over with the spirit of poetry that one was hardly conscious of any lack in their outward form. This critic claimed to be often surprised on studying the construction of a verse to find that it contained no rhyme at all, yet, he said, "I had not missed it, so beautiful was the thought, so expressive the diction, and so musical the inward rhythm, though the outward might be faulty."[31] Another critic, writing for *Queen, The Lady's Newspaper* in London, experienced a similar response to the poetry, calling Dickinson's *Poems, First Series* "one of the most remarkable books of verse that has fallen into my hands. It is full of thought of the rarest kind, and of subtlest music, too, although her verse obeys no law. It seems as if Miss Dickinson was satisfied to have a song in her heart, and cared little into what words it fell."[32]

As might be expected, explicit negative commentary about Dickinson's lack of form was led by Andrew Lang, the previously cited London critic who vilified Dickinson at every opportunity. In an 1891 article he wrote for the *London Daily News* entitled "An American Sappho," Lang berates Dickinson's verse for its lack of form: "It is really next to impossible to see the merit of poetry like Miss Dickinson's. She had thought a great deal, she did little but think, yet the expression of her thought is immeasurably obscure, unmelodious, and recklessly willful."[33] An anonymous American critic concurred with Lang in this piece written for the *New York Commercial Advertiser*, which considers Dickinson's poetry to be without form, having "every mark of haste, incomplete knowledge of the language, lack of rhythm, and sown thick with impossible, distressing rhymes." In fact, the writer continued:

> Miss Dickinson never learned the fingering of her instrument, as pianists say. She was mastered by words and sounds. She did

not know the technique of verse. She never realized that poetry is an art, which must be satisfied. She is like one who says, 'I will compose a symphony,' and does not know the elements of music. Miss Dickinson had no ear for verse. Words made no music for her.[34]

Though countless other examples could be given of the ambiguity concerning form and substance in Dickinson's verse, the assessment of this ambiguity is expressed quite well in the *Concord* [N.H.] *People and Patriot.* In this article, Dickinson's poems are recognized as being so out of the common that they must be judged by their own rules, since the poet had no regard for the conventional concordance of rhymes nor did she observe rhythm in the ordinary sense. Yet, the article states, "the reader must feel that she somehow satisfied the inner soul of harmony. To her ear these poems must have been melodious, and that is the impression they leave on the sensitive mind, despite their deviation from common critical standards."[35]

Clearly, a significantly high number of the critical reviews written during the eighteen-nineties expressed sensitivity to the musical qualities of Dickinson's poetry. However, it is one of the ironies of literature that Dickinson's poetry should be viewed as so obviously lacking in poetic form by readers and reviewers during the last decade of the nineteenth century, while contemporary criticism finds Dickinson's form to be one of the most distinctive aspects of her poetry and one of the most constant standards by which her poetry can be gauged. The form in which Dickinson's "startling little poetic bombs were cast" was a musical one, and the following chapter elaborates on that theory.

CHAPTER IV

Musical Form of Dickinson's Poetry: Contemporary Perspectives

Deficiency of form was the chief critical complaint registered against Emily Dickinson's poetry during the final decade of the nineteenth century. This deficiency was one perceived by her first literary editors, Mabel Loomis Todd and Thomas Wentworth Higginson. In the preface to Dickinson's *Poems, First Series* (1890), Higginson stated that Dickinson's words and phrases are "often set in a seemingly whimsical or even rugged frame," and in his *Reader's History of American Literature* (1903), he asserted that "Emily Dickinson never quite succeeded in grasping the notion of the importance of poetic form." Todd, in the preface to *Poems, Second Series* (1891), sought to defend the lack of form in Dickinson's poetry, saying, "Like impressionist pictures, or Wagner's rugged music, the very absence of conventional form challenges attention." To Dickinson's contemporaries, and to most critics at the time her poems were posthumously published, her seemingly unpatterned verses appeared to be the work of an original but undisciplined artist. In actuality, however, Dickinson was creating "a new medium of poetic expression," according to Thomas H. Johnson, "one based on the metric forms familiar to her from childhood as the iambic, trochaic, and occasionally dactylic measures in which Isaac

Watts's hymns were composed."[1] Martha Winburn England's study of Emily Dickinson and Isaac Watts, in *Hymns Unbidden*, not only lends support to Johnson's statement but adds that "the formal influence in all of Dickinson's poetry is the hymn. When music is considered along with the hymn texts, that influence is seen as pervasive."[2] Thus, the musicality of Dickinson's poetry is further demonstrated by the fact that she chose a musical form as her chief poetic structuring device.

The primary source of information about Emily Dickinson's knowledge of hymns comes from the hymnals she used during the years she attended Amherst Academy, Mount Holyoke Seminary, and the Congregational Church. One of these hymn books was *The Psalms, Hymns, and Spiritual Songs of the Rev. Isaac Watts, D.D., to which are added, Select Hymns, from other Authors; and Directions for Musical Expression*. Known as *Watts & Select*, it was edited by Samuel Worcester and was first published in 1819. Other hymn books were *Church Psalmody ... Selected from Dr. Watts and Other Authors*, edited by Lowell Mason and David Green in 1831, and *Village Hymns ... A Supplement to Dr. Watts's Psalms and Hymns*, edited by Asahel Nettleton in 1824.[3] In addition, Dickinson could scarcely have avoided the influence of Isaac Watts's extremely popular *Divine Songs Attempted in Easy Language For ... Children*, a collection of hymns for children designed to provide moral instruction in such a way as to capture their interest rather than bore them with deep theology. Generations of eighteenth- and nineteenth-century children sang and memorized these verses, and Dickinson was no doubt one of them. From her earliest years, Dickinson's mind was inculcated with the words and the music of Isaac Watts's hymns, and it is small wonder that his influence on her own poetic form was so pervasive and enduring.

Dickinson's poetic structure, then, was derived from the Protestant hymn. Like Watts, Dickinson favored the Common Hymn Meter as her basic pattern, and Charles Anderson considers this to be perhaps the finest stroke of Emily Dickinson's wit. He observes, "Though the form went back at least three hundred years before her day as the standard of English hymnology, it offered the immediate advantage of novelty, since no poet had ever exploited it fully as a serious verse form." Anderson contends that choosing such a "primitive lute" for her "sophisticated devotionals" was characteristic of her strategy, for most of her poems, too, "were hymns in their own special way."[4] Dickinson wrote nineteenth-century hymns, which differed from those of Watts's eighteenth-century hymns "by their general metrical freedom, freer use of enjambment, and use of more images with no scriptural references."[5]

Because she used the hymn forms with such rhythmic subtleties, the formal sources of Dickinson's poetry were mostly unnoticed until Thomas Johnson's discussion in his 1955 interpretative biography of Emily Dickinson. Here Johnson commented on the significance of the fact that every poem Dickinson composed before 1861, during the years she was learning her craft, is fashioned in Common Meter, Long Meter or Short Meter, the principal iambic meters which accompany each song in Isaac Watts's hymn books. Her early preference was for Common Meter, so by the time she began to use the various meters, she demonstrated her ability to create an innovative style of her own. Johnson believes Dickinson's greatest contribution to English prosody was that she perceived how to gain new effects by exploring the possibilities within traditional metric patterns and by eventually merging in one poem the various meters themselves. By this process, "the forms, which intrinsically carry their own retardment or acceleration, could be made to supply the continuum for the mood and ideas of the language."[6] As David Porter has noted, "Dickinson required a shape and a rhythm to hold her words and, along with literary Protestantism, the nineteenth century handed it to her."[7]

Other contemporary critics have comprehended the importance of Dickinson's acquisition of the hymn meter to establish the structure for her verse. In his study of Dickinson and her culture, Barton Levi St. Armand says that "... the sing-song lines of common meter, long meter, and short meter reverberated in her mind and in her art almost until the day of her death."[8] Martha England finds that Emily Dickinson and Isaac Watts were well matched as metrists, "with delicate ears for nuance, sensitive awareness of musical conventions absorbed from childhood on, and audacity to revolutionize a metrical situation."[9] In summary, the hymn was for Dickinson "the way words grouped themselves, established their bonds, and took their cadence in her mind."[10]

These observations gain validity when they are compared to common musical and poetical practices of Dickinson's time. For example, the majority of nineteenth-century hymn books contained no music at all, only lyric verses (hymns), which were labeled according to their meter. The metrical index for these hymns included these three most commonly used meters: Common Meter, with a pattern of 8.6.8.6. syllables per line; Short Meter, whose pattern is 6.6.8.6. syllables; and Long Meter, which contains 8.8.8.8. syllables in each line. As Joseph Jones has said, "This convenient classification and register of hymn-tune meters enabled a congregation to achieve extensive variety by singing a given set of words to any of several tunes."[11] It also served as a convenient pattern for Dickinson to adopt for the structure of her poetry.

Also, during Dickinson's school days poetry was taught from rhetoric books which emphasized musical analogies. The margins of Emily Dickinson's hymnbooks give standard markings to indicate expression in musical terms, and the marks relate to words, for no music is printed in the books. According to Martha England, the relationship of these marks to the markings in Dickinson's manuscripts have never been investigated, but it is agreed that "her markings indicate some sort of directions for expression, in addition to or instead of grammatical punctuation."[12]

Considerable speculation has surrounded Dickinson's unusual punctuation, particularly her frequent, and seemingly quirky, use of the dash. That, too, may be traced to the structure of the hymn books of her day. In his book *The Art of Emily Dickinson's Early Poetry*, David Porter provides an excerpt from the preface of Watts's *Psalms, Hymns, and Spiritual Songs* which offers opportunity for speculation on the correlation of Dickinson's utilization of the dash in relation to the same technique in hymn writing. In this preface, the editor, the Reverend Mr. Samuel Worcester, offers the following instruction:

> In the *punctuation* regard has been had to musical expression.
> In some instances, therefore, different points or pauses are
> inserted, from what would have been used, had the grammatical
> construction, only, been regarded. The *dash* is intended to
> denote an expressive suspension. In order to good expression,
> a distinct and judicious observation of the pauses is absolutely
> necessary.[13]

Thomas Johnson considers that Dickinson's use of the dash within lines often has no grammatical function, but, instead, "… is rather a visual representation of a musical beat."[14] St. Armand speculates that the "representative psalms, gospel passages, and prayers marked with a special notation of bars and dashes" in Edward Dickinson's hymnal, *Sabbath Hymn Book of 1858*, "may have had great relevance for the idiosyncratic punctuation of Dickinson's poems.[15]

With hymn pages that looked like pages of lyric poetry and with punctuation designed to denote expressive musical suspension, it is little wonder that Dickinson came naturally to depend on the standard hymn stanza for the framework in which to set her words. Albert Gelpi observes that "like a good American craftsman, Dickinson whittled her materials, within the limits of a rather strict form, into something of beauty and use."[16] For the form in which to set her words, Dickinson chose the standard hymn stanzas to "create a new, often staccato music of her own."[17] Dickinson, through this process, proves Martha England's thesis that "a lyric poet stores in the recesses of being some idea of form that must be satisfied."[18]

The hymn form, however, severely constrained Dickinson's verse and what she was able to perceive with it "even as she invested that narrow shape with intimate and unsurpassed power." Dickinson's strict reliance on the hymn form, adds Porter, "reveals with new clarity the severe limits of her compositional craft," yet, "with all its constraints and narrow vision, Dickinson never abandoned the hymn."[19] Indeed, the art of Dickinson's poetry, according to St. Armand, lies in its strict adherence to hymn forms. This consistency, he claims, "allowed Dickinson to condense and abstract complex motifs as she fitted them to the purposely limited requirements of her art, as rigid as the geometric patterns dictated for patchwork quilts."[20] Jane Eberwein sums these ideas up quite well by stating, "Not cathedral tunes, symphonies, or even natural sounds guided her verse forms but the familiar, simple melodies of American hymns—though even in borrowing these hymn measures she adapted them mainly in compression."[21] In her best poems, asserts Charles Anderson, she "made the form so completely her own that the singsong of the traditional hymn has been absorbed into a flexible modern instrument of infinite skills."[22] She took the hymn tune and made it her own as she "reduced her complicated meanings to fit Watts's simple structures."[23]

Dickinson wrote what she herself called "hymns," and, though the nineteenth-century critics did not perceive the structural connection of Dickinson's poetry to standard nineteenth-century hymns, one writer of that period detected the essence of the connection when he wrote that her "poems are like strains of solemn music floating at night from some wayside church. Each thought is complete and rare, solemn with a solemnity of intense conviction and calm with the calm of the deep-toned vibrating church bell."[24] Discovery of the relationship between Dickinson's poetry and the hymn form awaited the twentieth-century critics, who have found that relationship to be an inseparable one.

Dickinson was highly innovative and far ahead of her time when she chose to mold her profound poetic thoughts into the humble hymn form. Indeed, it would be almost a century after her death before a book-length study on the intimate kinship between poems and hymn-tunes in general would be published. Joseph Jones wrote this work, *Poems and Hymn-Tunes as Songs: Metrical Partners*, in order to establish the relationship inherent in this combination. He created a manual and cassette package which is designed to review the essential verse forms, to describe and demonstrate the metrical indexes found in most hymnals, and then to present a series of illustrations—songs made from poems set to hymn-tunes, employing several different poems and meters. It is worthwhile to examine his work in the light of Dickinson's adaptation of the hymn form for her poetry, for it confirms the intimate relationship which she perceived between poetry and the hymn-tune. Jones explains his purpose and methodology in this way:

> When we add music to verse we see the poet's achievement in a new perspective.... We now hear the poem in a different context, literally as never before. Most important of all, perhaps, we have undertaken for ourselves the role of performer—a role moreover in which we act simultaneously as performer and audience. Not only have we given the poem a new dress; we have placed ourselves in a new and more responsive relation to it. For all this, the hymn-tune is the most flexible, most readily accessible musical form.[25]

Though Jones matched the poetic rhythms of numerous poets with music in this study, he was especially drawn to Emily Dickinson's poetry because it so abundantly manifested her adaptations of, and variations upon, the metres of the humble church-hymn. For instance, in *A Garland for Emily. Twenty Songs by Emily Dickinson*, Jones set twenty of Dickinson's poems to period hymn-tunes ranging in origin from the sixteenth century to Emily Dickinson's own lifetime. Jones believes that Dickinson would have been familiar with a fair share of the hymn-tunes he uses. He concludes, "In singing or listening to such combinations as these, we make ourselves doubly aware of how closely related, in certain personalities, music and poetry have been and continue to be."[26]

Scholars are in general agreement about the close relationship existing between the hymn form and Dickinson's poetry. Since Dickinson derived her stanza forms so exclusively from the Congregational hymns, James Davidson wonders if she was also influenced by the content and style of the hymns: "If the architecture appealed to her, one may be certain that the message did, too."[27] Whether the message appealed to Dickinson or repelled her has generated considerable speculation from such scholars as Shira Wolosky, Charles Anderson, David Porter, and Judy Jo Small. While this is a question that remains unresolved at the present time, it is appropriate to present the studies which two musical arrangers are currently undertaking in an effort to substantiate the correlation between Dickinson's poetry and the content and style of hymns, particularly those of Isaac Watts.

One of these arrangers, John A. Gould, an English professor at Phillips Academy in Andover, Massachusetts, shared some of the methods he has used to effectively demonstrate the study of metrical structure to his students by taking popular hymns and singing poems by Emily Dickinson to them. He and some of his colleagues performed these songs *a cappella* in front of their English classes to illustrate for them the properties of meter, the relationship between Dickinson's poems and hymns, and the nature of sung poetry. "Meter is poetry's link with music," Gould says, and he believes that this practical application of prosody relieves the students from the mechanical instruction of metrical terms and patterns while also often lending vitality to the meaning. For example, Dickinson's poem "Abraham to kill him" (P 1317) is iconoclastic enough without reference to meter, according to Gould, "but when it is sung to the tune of 'Onward, Christian Soldiers,' it becomes delightfully blasphemous," as does "I heard a fly buzz when I died" (P 465) when it is set to Luther's grand old hymn, "A Mighty Fortress is Our God." Gould was particularly touched with Dickinson's "The Red Blaze in the Morning" (P 469) when it was set in the common meter of "Aurelia," which is also the tune for "The Church's One Foundation." He says, "It certainly was true that the meaning—which for poetry I think is both emotional and intellectual apprehension—emerged like a freight train from the singing of that poem. I know that music can do this for poetry."[28] By putting Dickinson's poetry into the framework of familiar hymns, Gould and his colleagues believe that they are successfully bringing to students an awareness of the musical nature of lyric poetry as the "young prosodists" discover that rhythm is what makes it all possible. One young critic found that the singers "were very interesting to listen to because of the way they took the rhythm of poems and put it to music," and Gould finds that in the phrase "the rhythm of poems," the point had been made.

The other arranger interested in establishing a relationship between Dickinson's poetry and the hymn-tune is Noel Tipton, a graduate of the Julliard School of Music. Tipton reveals that he, too, has found some innovative ways in which Dickinson's poetry and hymn tunes can be compared. For instance, when Tipton discovered the Dickinson verse, "Rearrange a Wife's Affection" (P 1737), he claims that "the words leapt off the page and burst into song" to the Nettleton tune of "Come Thou Fount of Every Blessing." When he sang the Dickinson verse to that tune, he found that he had an immediate grasp of the meaning of the verse which his later reading about Emily Dickinson confirmed to be correct. He said, "The tune/verse relationship fascinated me and spurred the thought that Dickinson, either consciously, sub-consciously or unconsciously had been influenced by this tune when she composed her verse." However, when Tipton looked for references to the tunes which accompanied the hymns she knew, he found only a void. Of this void, Tipton says, "Knowing something about the power of melody, rhythm and beat as a form of therapy in releasing conflicted emotions and thought, *vis-a-vis* the lyric writing process, it seemed plausible that Emily Dickinson's verses should be looked at from that point of view." Thus began his fascinating and ongoing project.

The question Tipton has proposed to Dickinson scholars is this: "Did the hymn tunes also contribute to Dickinson's creative process?" The response from these scholars has been that the meters and the doctrines set forth in certain hymns undoubtedly had influenced her, but beyond that no research has been forthcoming. To this all but universal acceptance of the influence of the hymn tune as the metric model for Dickinson's verses, Tipton adds the thought that hymns were written to be sung, and, he says, "although the tunes did vary according to the song leaders, the important point is that they were *sung*, not read. Singing gives the word a different slant and alters the feeling it evokes." Because Dickinson was a creative person with educated, sensitive musical responses, it seems worth considering, according to Tipton, that the tunes also exerted some influence on her.

In light of that consideration, Tipton suggests that the Dickinson verses he has found and set to music take on deeper meaning and resonance when *sung* to certain tunes. One such verse is "A dying tiger moaned for drink" (P 566). In trying to discover why it sings so well, Tipton searched for a tune which expressed its meaning and which was attached to a related verse. The two tunes he discovered from this period which fit the dramatic flow of the text were "Bangor" and "Martyrdom." Both tunes were used with the Watts hymn "Alas, and Did My Savior Bleed," but Tipton chose "Martyrdom" to illustrate his theory. By placing the Watts and Dickinson works side by side, Tipton made comparisons which further establish the relationship between Dickinson's poetry and Isaac Watts's hymns. He found that they have things in common beyond general theme. For example, Tipton's experiment revealed that the "melodic contour and the metric emphasis" of the hymn-tune matches the "shape and meaning of the verse," thus enhancing the value of both. Tipton concedes that we may never know positively whether Emily Dickinson was influenced, consciously or unconsciously, by the tunes to the hymns she knew so well, but he is convinced that certain of these tunes do color some of her verses with a different light. Tipton says, "The power of melody to move, to heal and to inspire on a poetic, creative and/or psychological level is indisputable. That it may relate to the work of Emily Dickinson through the serendipity of hymn tunes is intriguing and exciting."[29]

Beginning with the power of Isaac Watts's melodies, which permeated life from cradle to grave in Dickinson's Connecticut River Valley, these melodies became such an integral part of Dickinson's being that they eventually became transposed into an element of the literary form she created for her lyric verse. Though the nineteenth century failed to detect this relationship, contemporary scholars have all but universally accepted the connection which exists between Isaac Watts's hymn-tunes and the musical form of Dickinson's poetry. By placing some of Dickinson's poems back into the hymn-tunes from which they might have been derived, it may be possible to gain greater understanding and meaning from the poems, thus completing the circle from Watts to Dickinson and back to Watts, and other well known hymnists, again.

CHAPTER V

Musical Meters in Dickinson's "Hymns"

By adapting the hymn form to fit her complex and often enigmatic thoughts and by turning it to new use, Dickinson not only became a great poet but an accomplished metrist and hymnist as well. She often referred to her own poems as "hymns." On one notably rare occasion, Dickinson agreed to donate some of her poems to a charitable organization in Amherst. Uncertain of which poems to select, she wrote to T. W. Higginson, requesting his advice: "I have promised three Hymns to a charity, but without your approval could not give them — They are short and I could write them quite plainly, and if you felt it convenient to tell me if they were faithful, I should be most grateful..." (L 674). In another instance, Dickinson sent this brief message to her cousin Louise Norcross: "Brother has visited, and the night is falling, so I must close with a little hymn," which was her poem "This was in the white of the year" (L 307). Dickinson's penchant for including poems in her letters was a life-long custom. Very often, her poems expanded on the prose subject of the letter, and many of them were composed precisely with that intent. Others were included simply because she wanted to share her hymns with family and friends. For Dickinson, the words "poem" and "hymn" were often interchangeable, and it is clear that she thought of her own poems as hymns.

Dickinson often referred to poetry written by other poets as "hymns," also. For example, when Dickinson wrote to Higginson after her father's death to thank him for his kind remembrance of her family, she added, "Your beautiful Hymn, was it not prophetic? It has assisted the Pause of Space which I call 'Father'" (L 418). The hymn of which she speaks was Higginson's poem "Decoration," a poem appropriate for Memorial Day. In another illustration, Dickinson refers to James Russell Lowell's poem *After the Burial* as his "Slipper Hymn" because of the poignant last stanza depicting "That little shoe in the corner / So worn and wrinkled and brown," a description of a "slipper" once belonging to a now departed child (L 622). And, after quoting two lines from Alfred Lord Tennyson, one from *In Memoriam* and the other from *Love and Duty*, Dickinson wrote Mrs. Holland that they were "Both in the same Book — in the same Hymn —" (L 801).

Dickinson chose the word "hymn" as a means of expression in several of her poems. In one, she describes the blue jay's loud, harsh call as "Bold as a Bailiff's Hymn —" in one version and "Good as a Norseman's Hymn" (P 1177) in another. The songs of the faithful which extend into eternity she alludes to in another poem as the "Clear strains of Hymn / The River could not drown —" (P 260). In another instance, Dickinson's attempt to describe the heavenly music she hears is so futile that she resorts to what it is *not*, as in "It is not Hymn from pulpit read" (P 157).

One poem relates how the poet consoles a desperately ill friend, and in her effort to comfort and uplift him, she "sang firm — even — Chants —" which "helped his Film — with Hymn —" (P 616). The consolation provided there is not evident in another poem where she claims to be ignorant "Of pretty ways of Covenant — / How awkward at the Hymn" (P 944). One poem, depicting a masculine and a feminine side of the poet's personality, alludes to unspecified fears which beset the two. As a coping strategy to calm their anxiety, Tim, the masculine side, "reads a little Hymn — / And we both pray" (P 196). And, finally, in a poem which promotes the cultivation of one's own acquaintance, the poet asserts that such a discovery would provide better entertainment "Than could Border Ballad — / Or Biscayan Hymn —" (P 746).

Allusions to hymns occur even more frequently in Dickinson's letters, where quoted portions of hymns are included to complement her thoughts or to illustrate her emotional condition. Though she did not always recall the words exactly, the intended sentiment was always retained, and these references provide insightful clues to the importance of hymns in Dickinson's life. In a letter to Mrs. J. G. Holland, for instance, Dickinson writes, "How precious Thought and Speech are! 'A present so divine,' was in a Hymn they used to sing when I went to Church" (L 521). She was no doubt recalling lines from the last stanza of Isaac Watts's hymn, "When I Survey the Wondrous Cross," which reads: "Were the whole realm of nature mine, / That were a present far too small." These lines from the hymn help Dickinson illustrate how "precious" she considers thought and speech to be. In an 1852 letter to Susan Gilbert, Dickinson extrapolates in a humorous vein on the wondrous ways of God with man, the natural progression of which leads her to quote a portion of William Cowper's hymn, "Light Shining out of Darkness": "God moves in a mysterious way, his wonders to perform, he plants his foot upon the sea, and rides upon the storm" (L 97). That she was quoting from memory is suggested by the slight adjustment she made in Cowper's original words, "He plants his footsteps in the sea," thus creating a subtle change more suitable to her own metrical sense. In another letter to Susan, Dickinson takes some lines from the second stanza of a hymn by James Montgomery which read: "'Tis not the whole of life to live; / Nor all of death to die," paraphrasing these words to say, "Not all of life to live, is it, nor all of death to die" (L 176). Another James Montgomery hymn had special significance for Dickinson, for it was, she said, almost the last hymn her father heard before his death (L 414). The hymn, entitled "Rest from Thy Loved Employ," contains words which Dickinson considers to be an appropriate epitaph for her beloved father, and she quotes them as such in a letter to her Norcross cousins:

> Servant of God, well done!
> Rest from thy loved employ.
> The battle fought, the victory won,
> Enter thy Master's joy!

Samuel Bowles's death prompted the recollection of another hymn, and on the afternoon of his burial, Dickinson wrote to Higginson about "the last song that I heard — that was since the Birds — was 'He leadeth me — he leadeth me — yea, though I walk'" (L 533). Here Dickinson combines "He Leadeth Me," a hymn based on Psalm 23, with the solo piece, "The Twenty-Third Psalm," which Nora Green sang for a special occasion at First Church and later sang at the Homestead while Emily and Lavinia listened from upstairs.

Dickinson's interest in hymns can be traced throughout her letters, and this interest, coupled with Dickinson's participation in hymnsinging, particularly during her formative years, provides ample evidence of the importance of hymnody to Emily Dickinson. Even before she quit going to church by the age of thirty, she would sit "out in the new grass" of the Homestead lawn some Sunday mornings to listen "to the anthems" (L 184) from the First Congregational Church just across the street, vicariously participating in the service of music. From the open windows of First Church, she would have heard strains of hymns representing all periods of church song, and, as she was known to do when she attended church, she was perhaps inspired on these occasions to make up new words to match the meters of the hymns. She would have heard the hymns of James Montgomery, William Cowper, Charles Wesley, Timothy Dwight, and other well-known hymn writers, and she was no doubt influenced by them, though Watts's hymns predominate overall. The biblical themes which these hymn writers developed became topics for many of Dickinson's own hymns as well. It is the purpose of this chapter to examine the skill with which Dickinson transformed these topics into her hymns while simultaneously blending her poetic meters with some of the familiar hymns of her day.

A word should be said here about meter as it applies to both music and poetry in order to assess Dickinson's metrical skill more clearly. Meter connotes rhythm in verse by indicating the measured, patterned arrangement of syllables in a line of poetry, primarily according to stress and length. It is the recurrence in poetry of a rhythmic pattern. Meter also determines rhythm in music, especially the division of that rhythm into measures having a uniform number of beats. Meter provides structure whereas rhythm provides movement within the structure. Many critics find successful movement within a structured medium to be the chief index of poetic accomplishment because it is a double test of verbal skill to select meaningful words which simultaneously fall under a distinct principle of order. Recognition of this heightened order is widely considered to be a legitimate criterion for literary evaluation.[1]

By positioning a selected group of Dickinson's poems near the hymns whose meters match the poems, it is possible to see the metrical skill she employed to tailor her poems to fit the strict musical meters of the hymns. The hymns chosen for this purpose are eighteenth- and nineteenth-century hymns, and they have a variety of meters. The numbers which follow the meter name indicate the number of syllables in each line, for example: Common Meter (CM) 8.6.8.6. and Common Meter Double (CMD) 8.6.8.6.8.6.8.6.; Short Meter (SM) 6.6.8.6. and Short Meter Double (SMD) 6.6.8.6.6.6.8.6.; Long Meter (LM) 8.8.8.8. and Long Meter Double (LMD) 8.8.8.8.8.8.8.8. The blending of Dickinson's poems with these selected hymns should indicate the magnitude of the influence of hymn meter on Dickinson's poetry. The blending of poem to hymn is sometimes so startlingly beautiful it would seem that Dickinson surely must have had that particular hymn in her mind when she composed the poem.

This chapter, then, could be considered a "hymnal," for it is a collection of some of Dickinson's "hymns," all of which demonstrate that Dickinson was a consummate metrist. Because of the inherent religious nature of hymns, it is appropriate to focus on a selected group of Dickinson's poems which contain spiritual themes. The poems selected are all religious in nature, though some of them fit that category in distinctly unorthodox ways. These poems deal with subjects which can be found in the Topical Index at the back of any standard hymnal: God and Jesus; the Bible; Faith; Death; Immortality; and Joy. Each poem is quoted in its entirety, and the hymn which complements it immediately precedes it or shortly follows thereafter. Comments which precede the poems reflect Dickinson's own attitudes on each subject as they are revealed in her personal letters. Brief annotations on the hymns and the composers are included, also.

God and Jesus

The poem "Who were 'the Father and the Son'" tells much about Dickinson's past and present conceptions of the Deity. Her early letters are filled with accounts of painful struggles to accept Christ as her Savior and to give herself whole-heartedly to God, as so many friends and family members had already done. At one point Dickinson believed she had committed herself to God and she enjoyed "perfect peace and happiness" during that short period of time in which she felt she had "found her savior" (L 10). That euphoria did not last, however, and much of Dickinson's poetry concerns the search to replace that coveted sense of contentment. Dickinson's quest to know who *were* "the Father and the Son" expresses her childhood desire to consider carefully and ponder deeply a spiritual relationship for which she received no satisfactory explanations. As an adult, the poet believes that this same quest to know who *are* "the Father and the Son" would be answered by the Father and the Son *himself.* Yet, she grieves the lost years of friendship and the vacillation of belief, as Poem 1258 indicates:

> Who were "the Father and the Son"
> We pondered when a child,
> And what had they to do with us
> And when portentous told
>
> With inference appalling
> By Childhood fortified
> We thought, at least they are no worse
> Than they have been described.
>
> Who are "the Father and the Son"
> Did we demand Today
> "The Father and the Son" himself
> Would doubtless specify —
>
> But had they the felicity
> When we desired to know,
> We better Friends had been, perhaps,
> Than time ensue to be —

> We start — to learn that we believe
> But once — entirely —
> Belief, it does not fit so well
> When altered frequently —
>
> We blush, that Heaven if we achieve —
> Event ineffable —
> We shall have shunned until ashamed
> To own the Miracle —

Most appropriately, this poem about "the Father and the Son" fits the meter of a well-known Christmas carol, "O Little Town of Bethlehem," written by the Episcopal Bishop Phillips Brooks (1835–1893). The words were written in 1867, but the inspiration for them resulted from a trip Brooks took to the Holy Land in 1865, during which he made a horseback journey from Jerusalem to Bethlehem, where he assisted with the midnight service on Christmas Eve at the Basilica of the Nativity. The tune came to Lewis H. Redner, Brooks's organist at Holy Trinity Church in Philadelphia, on Christmas Eve in 1868, and was first sung the next day. The hymn tune is St. Louis, written in Common Meter Double (8.6.8.6.8.6.8.6.).

Truth was one of the attributes of God which Dickinson cherished, for truth was significantly important to her. Among the things Higginson remembered Emily Dickinson telling him on his first visit to the Homestead on August 16, 1870, was "Truth is such a *rare* thing it is delightful to tell it" (L 342a). Later, in a letter to Higginson praising the poems of Mrs. Hunt, Mrs. Browning, and Mrs. Lewes, Dickinson concludes that their individual talents should be acknowledged, for, she says, "truth like Ancestor's Brocades can stand alone —" (L 368). Dickinson honored truth, believing that "the quicker deceit dies, the better for the truth, who is indeed our dear friend" (L 357). Her high opinion of truth is exemplified by its comparison to God as "His twin identity" in Poem 836:

> Truth — is as old as God —
> His Twin identity
> And will endure as long as He
> A Co-Eternity —

O Little Town of Bethlehem

And perish on the Day
Himself is borne away
From Mansion of the Universe
A lifeless Deity.

Timothy Dwight (1752–1817), president of Yale, one of the leading preachers of the Second Great Awakening, and a grandson of
Jonathan Edwards, wrote the words to "I Love Thy Kingdom, Lord,"

I Love Thy Kingdom, Lord

the last line of which reads "Sure as Thy truth shall last." This hymn was included in *Psalms of David* in 1800 and is believed to be the oldest hymn by an American that is still in common use. The hymn tune is St. Thomas, written in Short Meter (6.6.8.6.) by Aaron Williams and included in *The New Universal Psalmodist*, 1770. Lyman Beecher, a friend of the Dickinson family, was a student of Timothy Dwight's at Yale. It is highly unlikely that Emily Dickinson was unaware of this hymn that complements her poem so well.

Jealousy was a trait of God which caused Dickinson frequent and genuine trepidation, especially because she feared that God would take away her loved ones if she cherished them above him. She would have been familiar with the numerous passages in the Bible about God's jealousy. As Exodus 20:3 states, "I the Lord your God am a jealous God," while Moses' words to Israel before they passed into the Promised Land express this thought in even stronger terms in Deuteronomy 4:24: "For the Lord thy God is a consuming fire, *even* a jealous God." And, most of all, Dickinson would have known that the Ten Commandments forbids having other gods before God, and Dickinson's adoration of her friends bordered on just such idolatry. Recognizing this fact, Dickinson hoped that one day God would

O FOR A CLOSER WALK WITH GOD

restore her "confiscated gods," those whom she had loved perhaps too much so that God had taken them away. She confessed that her friends were her "estate" in a letter to Samuel Bowles, adding, "Forgive me then the avarice to hoard them! ... God is not so wary as we, else he would give us no friends, lest we forget him!" (L 193). She expresses this sentiment succinctly in Poem 1719:

> God is indeed a jealous God —
> He cannot bear to see
> That we had rather not with Him
> But with each other play.

The English poet William Cowper (1731–1800) wrote the words to "O For A Closer Walk With God," which matches quite well with this short poem. The hymn was included in Conyer's *Collection of*

Psalms and Hymns, 1772. John B. Dykes wrote the tune for this hymn which is Beatitudo written in Common Meter (8.6.8.6.). Cowper's poems were in the library at the Homestead, and Dickinson undoubtedly was acquainted with his poetry and his hymns.

The most significant point to acknowledge about this poet's religious posture, as Eberwein has noted, is that "God was the most important person in Emily Dickinson's life, and her relationship with him excelled all others in endurance and intensity."[2] Yet Dickinson's attitudes toward God went through periods of modulation, from her apprehension of God's jealousy to her recognition that "God is good" (L 93) and "loving and kind" (L 166). While Dickinson recognizes many of the worthy qualities of God, he often seems remote to her, "a distant — stately Lover" (P 357) who appears to be much more friendly at a distance "through a hearty Lens" (L 492).

In contrast, Dickinson identifies with Christ, more so because of his humanity than his divinity. She even concludes, in a letter to Higginson, that "To be human is more than to be divine, for when Christ was divine, he was uncontented till he had been human (L 519). The following poem indicates that Dickinson comprehends the vital role played by Christ in his Incarnation. One of the few poems to have a title, Dickinson called it "Christ's Birthday" when she sent it to Higginson in 1880, along with three other poems, soliciting his approval for her "three Hymns to charity." In this simple poem (P 1487), she captures Christ's mission to the world:

> The Savior must have been
> A docile Gentleman —
> To come so far so cold a Day
> For little Fellowmen —
>
> The Road to Bethlehem
> Since He and I were Boys
> Was leveled, but for that 'twould be
> A rugged billion Miles —

"We Give Thee But Thine Own," written in 1864 by William W. How (1823–1897), complements this poem beautifully. The hymn tune is Schumann in Short Meter (6.6.8.6.) and was in Lowell Mason & George J. Webb's *Cantica Laudis,* 1850.

WE GIVE THEE BUT THINE OWN

Dickinson applies the Incarnation to the human condition in another poem, asserting that Christ, as forerunner, has already traveled the road leading from death to life eternal. Therefore, "No New Mile remaineth," she writes, for Christ, as "Tender Pioneer" (P 698), blazed the way for others to follow, thus eliminating the fear of death so inherent in the human condition. Christ's willingness to accept the "Crown of Thorns" in his substitutionary death on the cross "deified" the "stigma" which such an infamous death would ordinarily connote, according to Poem 1735:

> One crown that no one seeks
> And yet the highest head
> Its isolation coveted
> Its stigma deified
>
> While Pontius Pilate lives
> In whatsoever hell
> That coronation pierces him
> He recollects it well.

This poem is enhanced by matching it with "A Charge to Keep I Have," a hymn by Charles Wesley (1707–1788), who wrote

A Charge to Keep I Have

over 6,000 hymns. This hymn was included in *Short Hymns on Select Passages of Holy Scripture,* 1762. Lowell Mason (1792–1872) wrote the music to the Boylston hymn tune which is in Short Meter (6.6.8.6.).

Dickinson's understanding of the Trinity is evident in Poem 817. Though she speaks of the Father, the Son, and the Holy Ghost separately in other poems, here she joins them together in a significant poem wherein the speaker is identified as "Bride of the Father and the Son / Bride of the Holy Ghost." This poem, considered by some to be Dickinson's declaration of her status as the Bride of Christ, is in keeping with a quotation from Dickinson's favorite book of the Bible, the Book of Revelation, which speaks in chapter 21, verse 9 of the faithful church as the "bride" of Christ. In either case, Dickinson posits the superiority of the heavenly marriage over that of the earthly one.

> Given in Marriage unto Thee
> Oh thou Celestial Host —
> Bride of the Father and the Son
> Bride of the Holy Ghost.

Come, Holy Spirit, Heavenly Dove

Come, Ho-ly Spir - it, Heav'n - ly Dove, With all thy quick - 'ning pow'rs;

Kin-dle a flame of sa - cred love In these cold hearts of ours.

Other Betrothal shall dissolve —
Wedlock of Will, decay —
Only the Keeper of this Ring
Conquer Mortality —

Dickinson was profoundly influenced by Thomas à Kempis's classic work, *Of the Imitation of Christ,* which she received as a Christmas gift from her sister-in-law Susan in 1876. One chapter concerns the theme of eternal rest in Christ, and in it the speaker uses marriage imagery to express a relationship to Christ: "O thou most beloved spouse of my soul. Jesus Christ, thou most pure Lover," and then refers to Psalm 55: 6: "Oh that I had wings like a dove! For then would I fly away, and be at rest." Perhaps then, it is not by accident that this poem so aptly suits the Isaac Watts's hymn "Come, Holy Spirit, Heavenly Dove." The hymn was included in Watts's *Hymns and Sacred Songs,* 1707. The music was composed by John B. Dykes to the St. Agnes tune in Common Meter (8.6.8.6).

The Bible

That Dickinson possessed unusually thorough biblical knowledge, of both the Old and the New Testaments, is beyond conjecture. Indeed, her poems and letters are so liberally sprinkled with biblical quotations, allusions, and metaphors that consideration of these elements enlivens her work and illuminates the rich imagery she derived from the Scriptures. The Bible permeated her consciousness more than any other book and became a basis from which she expressed her deepest longings and her loftiest aspirations. Though she once considered the Bible to be an "arid book," when she began to read the Old and New Testaments in earnest, she saw "how infinitely wise & merry" it was.[3]

Dickinson drew "wise and merry" analogies to biblical stories in poem after poem and in letter after letter. In an 1847 letter to Austin, she demonstrates her knowledge of the story about the prophet Daniel, who interpreted dreams but was also thrown into the lions' den. Outlining a dream she had the previous night, she desires that Austin "turn Daniel and interpret it to me, or if you dont care about going through all the perils which he did I will allow you to interpret it without" (L 16). In a letter to her Norcross cousins, she interpolates Noah's sending the dove from the ark to search for dry land, returning on the third day with an olive leaf in this way: "Mother went rambling, and came in with a burdock on her shawl, so we know that the snow has perished from the earth. Noah would have liked mother" (L 339). And Mrs. J. G. Holland, Dickinson's diminutive friend, must have been pleased with this complement: "That you be with me annuls fear ... Smaller than David you clothe me with extreme Goliath" (L 318).

The Bible was far more to Dickinson than the "antique volume" she mentions in a poem she wrote for her ailing nephew Ned, granting him "Sanctuary Privileges" since he could not attend church. Though the first part of this poem presents the "arid" version often presented in the Puritan churches of her time, she senses it is not the biblical stories themselves but those who tell them who perplex and even repel the young people of the day. In her mind, if the stories had a more "warbling Teller — / All the Boys would come — / Orpheus'

Sermon captivated — / It did not condemn —" (P 1545). Perhaps Dickinson herself assumed the role of "warbling Teller," as the following two biblical accounts indicate. In one, Dickinson wonders at the moral of the Old Testament story in which Abraham is ordered by God to sacrifice his only son Isaac, which Abraham obediently sets out to do. Dickinson's version of the story in Poem 1317 questions the consequences which inequality of power promotes:

> Abraham to kill him
> Was distinctly told —
> Isaac was an Urchin —
> Abraham was old —
>
> Not a hesitation —
> Abraham complied —
> Flattered by Obeisance
> Tyranny demurred —
>
> Isaac — to his children
> Lived to tell the tale —
> Moral — with a Mastiff
> Manners may prevail.

This poem, which details Abraham's "marching orders" from God, is uniquely suited to the hymn "Onward, Christian Soldiers." Sabine Baring-Gould (1834–1924) wrote the hymn in 1865 as a marching song for children to move from one English village to another to attend church services. Sir Arthur S. Sullivan, of light opera fame, composed the tune to St. Gertrude, which has a unique meter (6.5.6.5.D) with refrain.

Dickinson turned to the fifth chapter of the book of Daniel to provide the setting for her accurate rendition of the mysterious "handwriting on the wall." This supernatural event occurred at King Belshazzar's defiant banquet at his palace in Babylon when he and his guests drank and ate from the holy vessels sacrilegiously taken from the temple of God in Jerusalem. "Belshazzar's Correspondent," God, delivers the message to Belshazzar that he has been "weighed on the scales and found wanting." In Poem 1459, Dickinson implies that our collective conscience can find us all "wanting," too:

ONWARD, CHRISTIAN SOLDIERS

Belshazzar had a Letter —
He never had but one —
Belshazzar's Correspondent
Concluded and begun
In that immortal Copy
The Conscience of us all
Can read without its Glasses
On Revelation's Wall —

96

THE CHURCH'S ONE FOUNDATION

THE CHURCH-'S ONE FOUN - DA - TION IS JE - SUS CHRIST HER LORD; SHE
IS HIS NEW CRE - A - TION BY WA - TER AND THE WORD: FROM
HEAV'N HE CAME AND SOUGHT HER TO BE HIS HO - LY BRIDE; WITH
HIS OWN BLOOD HE BOUGHT HER, AND FOR HER LIFE HE DIED.

The "Church's One Foundation" provides a fine context for this poem. Samuel J. Stone (1839–1900) wrote this hymn, which was included in *Lyra Fedelium: Twelve Hymns of the Twelve Articles of the Apostle's Creed*, 1866. Samuel S. Wesley (1810–1876) composed the hymn tune in 1864 to Aurelia, which is a distinctive meter (7.6.7.6.D).

Faith

Dickinson's own interpretations of the Bible set her at odds with certain church doctrines which represented carefully worked out principles or creeds advocated by the Puritan-based churches of her day. Commenting on a sermon Reverend Seelye preached on predestination at First Church, Dickinson offered this observation: "... I do not respect 'doctrines,' and did not listen to him, so I can neither praise, nor blame" (L 200). Faith, however, was altogether different for Dickinson and she had much to say about it in her letters, mentioning the word *faith* thirty-six times, and in her poems, forty-five times. She recognized how fragile faith can be, yet she believed constant testing increased faith rather than diminished it. For her, "To believe the final line of the Card would foreclose Faith — Faith is *Doubt*" (L 912). Though her prayers sometimes went unanswered, she understood that "'Seek and ye shall find' is the boon of faith" (L 830).

Dickinson shows an understanding of the biblical meaning of faith as early as age fifteen in this letter to Abiah Root. Here Dickinson paraphrases from the Bible for the first time in what would become a fixed form of expression in later letters. After telling Root she is going to learn to make bread the next day, she expresses the thought that she could keep house very well if she only knew how to cook. "But," she observes, "as long as I don't, my knowledge of housekeeping is about of as much use as faith without works, which you know we are told is dead." Dickinson asks Root to excuse her for quoting from Scripture (James 2:17) "... faith, if it hath not works, is dead ...," but, she adds, "it was so handy in this case I couldn't get along very well without it" (L 8).

In other instances, Dickinson expresses her understanding of the biblical definition of faith from Hebrews 11:1: "Now faith is the substance of things hoped for, the evidence of things not seen." She expands on this thought when she suggests that "We dignify our Faith, when we can cross the ocean with it, though most prefer ships" (L 209). And she chides the "doubting Thomas" of the Bible for not believing accounts of Christ's resurrection, suggesting that "Thomas' faith in Anatomy, was stronger than his faith in faith" (L 233).

Faith was defined in Dickinson's lexicon as "a rope or cable — as

COME, WE THAT LOVE THE LORD

a slender but tough and resilient filament or force connecting the faithful soul to God."[4] Dickinson finds a very poetic way to express that definition, as well as the biblical one, in Poem 915:

> Faith — is the Pierless Bridge
> Supporting what We see
> Unto the Scene that We do not —
> Too slender for the eye
>
> It bears the Soul as bold
> As it were rocked in Steel
> With Arms of Steel at either side —
> It joins — behind the Veil
>
> To what, could We presume
> The Bridge would cease to be
> To Our far, vacillating Feet
> A first Necessity.

An Isaac Watts hymn, "Come, We That Love the Lord," provides a complementary accompaniment to this poem. The music was composed by Aaron Williams to the St. Thomas tune in Short

Meter (6.6.8.6.) and was included in *The New Universal Psalmodist*, 1770.

Dickinson's convictions about the significance of faith can be found in several poems. In one, she proclaims, "My Faith is larger than the Hills—" (P 766), and in another she testifies that "What I see not, I better see — / Through Faith —" (P 939). To emphasize the importance of faith, Dickinson asserts in Poem 377 that the loss of one's faith places an individual in a state of abject poverty:

> To lose one's faith — surpass
> The loss of an Estate —
> Because Estates can be
> Replenished — faith cannot —
>
> Inherited with Life —
> Belief — but once — can be —
> Annihilate a single clause —
> And Being's — Beggary —

This poem is enhanced by joining it with "Crown Him With Many Crowns," a hymn written by Matthew Bridges (1800–1894) and Godfrey Thring (1823–1903). The hymn tune, Diademata in Short Meter Double (6.6.8.6.6.6.8.6), was composed by George J. Elvey.

Death

Some of Dickinson's finest poems are on the theme of death. Though some are morbid, many are hopeful and even anticipatory of this event which befalls all of humanity. "Dying," Dickinson said, "is a wild Night and a new Road" (L 332), an occurrence signifying the end of one existence and the beginning of a far better one. Dickinson reiterated this belief often in her poems and letters. For instance, in a letter of sympathy to her cousin Perez Cowan, Dickinson affirms that he had lost his sister "through that sweeter Loss which we call Gain" (L 386). In another letter of consolation, this one to her Norcross cousins over the death of their father, Dickinson writes of the sweet reunion their father now has with their mother, who had preceded him in death: "The grief is our side, darlings, and the glad is

CROWN HIM WITH MANY CROWNS

CROWN HIM WITH MAN - Y CROWNS, THE LAMB UP - ON HIS THRONE: HARK!

HOW THE HEAV'N - LY AN - THEM DROWNS ALL MU - SIC BUT ITS OWN! A -

WAKE, MY SOUL, AND SING OF HIM WHO DIED FOR THEE, AND

HAIL HIM AS THY MATCH - LESS KING THRU ALL E - TER - NI - TY.

theirs." It was on this occasion that Dickinson asks of her cousins, "Let Emily sing for you because she cannot pray." Her "song" for them began "It is not dying hurts us so, — / 'Tis living hurts us more" (L 278).

Dickinson's preoccupation with the subject of death is seen by some as macabre, when, in truth, she is simply reflecting on the very real presence of death as it touched the lives of her friends and family near and far. Her acquaintance with death came early as she lost young friends to various diseases of the day such as consumption, intestinal fever, typhoid fever, scarlet fever, and, most dreaded of all, cholera. During the time the Dickinson family lived on Pleasant Street, across the street from the town cemetery, the death rate among the young people in the small village of Amherst was appalling. From 1851 to 1854, when Emily was ages twenty-one to twenty-four, recorded deaths in Amherst included eighteen females in their teens or early twenties and eleven males in a similar age bracket. The deaths of so many of her contemporaries led Dickinson to have "awe for friends," for death, "striking sharp and early," caused her to hold her friends "in a brittle love — of more alarm, than peace" (L 280). A letter to her friend Jane Humphrey, written when Dickinson was twenty-two, reflects the times in which she was living, for she mentions many of those she had loved dearly who "are not upon Earth, this lovely Sabbath evening. Bye and bye we'll all be gone, Jennie, *does it seem* as if we would?" Dickinson then tried to imagine herself as dead:

> The other day I tried to think how I should look with my eyes shut, and a little white gown on, and a snowdrop on my breast; and I fancied I heard the neighbors stealing in so softly to look down in my face — so fast asleep — so still — (L 86).

Perhaps this anecdote served as the precursor for one of Dickinson's best known death poems, "I heard a Fly buzz — when I died —" (P 465):

> I heard a Fly buzz — when I died —
> The Stillness in the Room
> Was like the Stillness in the Air —
> Between the Heaves of Storm —
>
> The Eyes around — had wrung them dry —
> And Breaths were gathering firm
> For that last Onset — when the King
> Be witnessed — in the Room —
>
> I willed my Keepsakes — Signed away
> What portion of me be
> Assignable — and then it was
> There interposed a Fly —

O GOD, OUR HELP IN AGES PAST

With Blue — uncertain stumbling Buzz —
Between the light — and me —
And then the Windows failed — and then
I could not see to see —

Isaac Watts's hymn "O God, Our Help in Ages Past" is considered to be one of the grandest in the whole realm of English hymnody and serves as a solid accompaniment for this poem. Watts, who took the words from Psalm 90, included the hymn in *The Psalms of David, 1719*. William Croft (1678–1727), recognized as the foremost church musician of his time, wrote the music in 1708 to the St. Anne hymn tune in Common Meter (8.6.8.6.).

One of Dickinson's most anthologized poems, and arguably her most famous poem about death, is "Because I could not stop for Death." Fear of death has no part in this transitional journey from the finite world into infinity, and Dickinson expresses that lack of fear in more than one instance. For example, in Poem 608 she asks, "Afraid! Of whom am I afraid? / Not Death — for who is He? / The Porter of my Father's Lodge / As much abasheth me!" Death, according to Dickinson, is "as harmless as a Bee, except to those who run" (L 294). Yet, since death was an ever-present reality in Dickinson's world, she concludes that "where Death has been introduced, he frequently calls,

I Sing the Mighty Power of God

making it desirable to forestall his advances" (L 311). Those advances could not be "forestalled," however, even for one too occupied with the process of living to be concerned with death, a theme Dickinson develops in her most notable poem about death, Poem 712:

> Because I could not stop for Death —
> He kindly stopped for me —
> The Carriage held but just Ourselves —
> And Immortality.

We slowly drove — He knew no haste
And I had put away
My labor and my leisure too,
For His Civility —

We passed the School, where Children strove
At Recess — in the Ring —
We passed the Fields of Gazing Grain —
We passed the Setting Sun —

Or rather — He passed Us —
The Dews drew quivering and chill —
For only Gossamer, my Gown —
My Tippet — only Tulle —

We paused before a House that seemed
A Swelling of the Ground —
The Roof was scarcely visible —
The Cornice — in the Ground —

Since then — 'tis Centuries — and yet
Feels shorter than the Day
I first surmised the Horses' Heads
Were toward Eternity —

Another Isaac Watts hymn, "I Sing the Mighty Power of God," proves to be an unusually good accompaniment for this poem. Watts wrote this children's hymn to be included in his book of songs especially for young people, *Divine and Moral Songs for Children*, 1715. The hymn tune is Ellacombe written in Common Meter Double (8.6.8.6.8.6.8.6.).

Immortality

It was not death itself but what lies beyond death that intrigued Dickinson throughout her life. "That *Bareheaded life* — under the grass — worries one like a Wasp," she wrote to Samuel Bowles in 1860 (L 220). The enigma of immortality served as a flint for sparking the creation of some of Dickinson's finest poems and many of her most thoughtful letters. Immortality was, in Dickinson's own words, "the Flood subject" (L 319).

Dickinson's earliest impression of immortality was a negative one. When she was very young, she was taken to a funeral where she misinterpreted the clergyman's question, "Is the Arm of the Lord shortened that it cannot save?" (L 503), to indicate a doubt of immortality. The impression this made on her young mind was long-lasting. However, that early impression was tempered by a young man who studied law under Edward Dickinson. Benjamin Franklin Newton is credited as being the Preceptor who taught Emily about books, authors, nature, and, of greatest import, he taught her "that sublimer lesson, a faith in things unseen, and in a life again, nobler, and much more blessed —" (L 153). After his early death, Dickinson spoke of him as the friend who taught her Immortality, "but venturing too near, himself — he never returned" (L 261).

Dickinson's quest to ascertain the secrets of immortality was a life-long endeavor. Her belief in immortality strengthened with each loss of family members, friends, and neighbors, prompting Dickinson to observe that "Immortality as a guest is sacred, but when it becomes … a member of the family, the tie is more vivid…" (L 644). So vivid was this tie for Dickinson that she wrote her cousin Perez Cowan, "I suppose we are all thinking of Immortality, at times so stimulatedly that we cannot sleep" (L 332). Certainly this was a transcendent experience for Dickinson while she was in Cambridge undergoing treatment for an eye condition. Though her doctor had taken away her pen and she was only able to use her eyes for short periods of time, she nonetheless managed to write in pencil from her "Prison," where she made "Guests" for herself. Though separated from home and family, and with only her Norcross cousins in attendance, Dickinson does not appear to be lonely, for she is encapsulated in thoughts of Immortality, as she expresses in a poem she sent to Higginson from Cambridge that "The Only News I know / Is Bulletins all Day / From Immortality" (P 827).

The concept of immortality was never far from Dickinson's thoughts. When she was only twenty-six, she expressed these thoughts of immortality in a letter to her cousin John Graves: "It is a jolly thought to think that we can be Eternal … that we have each a *pair* of lives, and need not chary be, of the one that *now* is —" (L 184). She relates this same conviction twenty-two years later in a letter to Mrs. J. G. Holland: "How unspeakably sweet and solemn — that whatever await us of Doom or Home, we are mentally permanent," adding that "'It is finished' can never be said of us" (L 555). "The mind of the Heart must live," she declares, "if it's clerical part do not" (L 503).

The Reverend Charles Wadsworth was Dickinson's spiritual advisor for many years and his death in April of 1882 had a profound impact on Dickinson. He was, she said, her "closest earthly friend" (L 765), her "Shepherd from 'Little Girl' hood" (L 766), and she could not imagine a world without him. Following his death, Wadsworth's lifelong friend James D. Clark sent a collection of Wadsworth's sermons to Dickinson, sermons which she termed "a sorrowful Treasure." This kind gesture initiated a correspondence with James D. Clark until his death in 1883, when that correspondence was resumed by his younger brother Charles H. Clark. With no spiritual advisor available, Dickinson turned to Charles Clark for questions about eternal life, questions which she feared few could answer for sure. Her particular concern centered around the life of the spirit without the body, and in a letter to Charles Clark, dated mid–October of 1883, she inquired if the same thoughts disturbed him (L 872). In order to better illustrate her emotional quandary, she enclosed the following poem (P 1576):

> The Spirit lasts — but in what mode —
> Below, the Body speaks,
> But as the Spirit furnishes —
> Apart, it never talks —
> The Music in the Violin
> Does not emerge alone
> But Arm in Arm with Touch, yet Touch
> Alone — is not a Tune —
> The Spirit lurks within the Flesh
> Like Tides within the Sea
> That make the Water live, estranged
> What would the Either be?
> Does that know — now — or does it cease —
> That which to this is done,
> Resuming at a mutual date
> With every future one?

MY SHEPHERD WILL SUPPLY MY NEED

Arr. - Steve Kirby

Instinct pursues the Adamant,
Exacting this Reply —
Adversity if it may be, or
Wild Prosperity,
The Rumor's Gate was shut so tight
Before my Mind was sown,
Not even a Prognostic's Push
Could make a Dent thereon —

It would seem implausible that any hymn, or any song for that matter, could match the meter of this long poem. Yet, once again, an Isaac Watts hymn provides an unusually fine musical setting for the poem. "My Shepherd Will Supply My Need" is a hymn based on Psalm 23. The language of the lyrics, though inspired by the Psalm and following its general thought, is pure Watts. It was published in a collection by Watts entitled *The Psalms of David Imitated in the Language of the New Testament and Applied to the Christian State and Worship*, 1802. The hymn tune is Resignation, with arrangement by Steve Kirby. This American folk hymn tune first appeared in William Walker's *Southern Harmony*, 1835. The meter is Common Meter Double (8.6.8.6.8.6.8.6.).

Dickinson was convinced that the spirit lives on after death, but she was perplexed over the question of how we will recognize our loved ones in heaven without their earthly bodies. In her grief over her father's "lonely Life and his lonelier Death," she found that the only worthwhile thing left in life was her thoughts of immortality, saying, "Take all away — / The only thing worth larceny / Is left — the Immortality" (P 1365). Following her father's death, Dickinson claimed that she dreamed of her father every night, a different dream nightly, and during the day she found herself to be forgetful and distracted, constantly wondering where her father was and pondering, "Without any body, I keep thinking. What kind can that be?" (L 471).

Dickinson expresses a similar sentiment in a condolence letter to Perez Cowan, whose infant daughter Margaret had recently died. Dickinson proposes that the child may have come to show him Immortality, suggesting that "Her startling little flight would imply she did." Dickinson expresses the hope that we will retain enough of ourselves that our immortal bodies are recognizable, so that heaven "is not so unlike Earth that we shall miss the peculiar form — the Mold of the Bird —" (L 671). The poem Dickinson includes in this letter was apparently inspired by I Corinthians 15:35 which addresses the question of the spiritual body: "But some men will say, How are the dead raised up? And with what body do they come?" Dickinson's version of that question follows in Poem 1492:

O FOR A THOUSAND TONGUES TO SING

"And with what body do they come?" —
Then they *do* come — Rejoice!
What Door — What Hour — Run — run — My Soul!
Illuminate the House!
"Body!" Then real — a Face and Eyes —
To know that it is them! —
Paul knew the Man that knew the News —
He passed through Bethlehem —

"O For a Thousand Tongues To Sing" was written by Charles Wesley in 1739. He wrote this hymn to commemorate the first anniversary of his conversion to Christ, and, in its original version, it contained nineteen stanzas. The hymn first appeared in *Hymns and Sacred Poems* in 1740. Carl G. Glazer wrote the music in 1828 to the Azmon tune in Common Meter (8.6.8.6.), and it was arranged by Lowell Mason in 1839.

Joy

Joy is a division in the topical index of any standard hymnal, and it is an appropriate heading for the following three poems, all of which express happiness, great pleasure, gladness, and delight. The first poem, "Some Keep the Sabbath going to Church," was one of the few poems Dickinson's titled; she called the poem "My Sabbath." It was one of ten poems printed during Emily Dickinson's lifetime, all anonymously. The first printing was in *The Round Table*, a weekly newspaper published in New York by Dickinson's cousins, Henry E. and Charles H. Sweetser, who retained Dickinson's title. It was also one of the poems Dickinson sent to Higginson for his approval on three poems she had promised to charity. When it appeared in the first edition of Dickinson's poems in 1890, Colonel Higginson exercised his editorial privilege to title the poem, "A Service of Song."

Popular with readers from the first, this poem departs from the traditional worship of the day and may have been a basis for the charge of irreverence from some late nineteenth-century reviewers. Toward the end of her life, Mabel Loomis Todd, who perhaps understood Dickinson better than most, included this note to the reprinting of her introduction to the first edition of Dickinson's letters in *Letters of Emily Dickinson, New and Enlarged Edition*, published in 1931. Her note begins, "Incredible as it now seems, I had to wage a constant battle throughout all those early years against charges of [Dickinson's] irreverence."[5] In the original "Introductory" to *Letters of Emily Dickinson*, published in 1894, Todd attempted to avoid such criticism by confronting it beforehand. While acknowledging that Dickinson's forefathers were leaders in town and church who did not question the religious teaching of the time and were "strict and uncompromising in their piety," Todd found Emily Dickinson's "great disinclination for an exposition of the theology current during her childhood" to be a "matter for small wonder." To Todd, it seemed perfectly in keeping with Dickinson's personal piety, as the following words show:

> Reverence for accepted ways and forms, merely as such, seems
> entirely to have been left out of Emily's constitution. To her,
> God was not a far-away and dreary Power to be daily
> addressed — the great "Eclipse" of which she wrote — but
> He was near and familiar and pervasive. Her garden was full of
> His brightness and glory, the birds sang and the sky glowed
> because of Him. To shut herself out of the sunshine in a church,

dark, chilly, restricted, was rather to shut herself away from Him...."[6]

In his biography of Emily Dickinson, Richard Sewall called her "perhaps the most religious person in town,"[7] though her attendance at church services virtually ended by the time she was thirty. Excerpts from two of Dickinson's letters, both written when she was twenty-four, may provide clues to her gradual withdrawal from formal worship. In one letter, Dickinson relates an almost surrealistic account of some experiences she had during a Sunday service at First Church, a service she attended alone, in the absence of her father, mother, brother, sister, and her friend Susan Gilbert. Following the service, from the safety of her home, she wrote Susan of this ordeal in which she "sorely feared" her "life" was made a "victim." She described how "big and broad the aisle seemed, full huge enough before," as she "quaked slowly up — and reached my usual seat!" She believed people were staring at her, and to compensate for that uncomfortable feeling, she "discovered *nothing* up in the sky somewhere, and gazed intently at it, for quite a half an hour." This calmed her down, but after church, she "walked, ran, and turned precarious corners" to reach her home following the service, where, she said, "I whirled the merry key, and fairly danced for joy, to find myself *at home!*" (L 154). Surely this was not an uplifting spiritual occurrence for Dickinson but rather one of emotional and psychic trepidation. Though Dickinson's tendency to exaggerate circumstances in her letters must be taken into account, at the very least this incident was not a positive one.

In another instance, Dickinson wrote Dr. and Mrs. J. G. Holland about a service she attended where the guest minister preached about "death and judgment, and what would become of those, meaning Austin and me, who behaved improperly —." The sermon scared her, particularly because her father and Vinnie "looked very solemn as if the whole was true," but Dickinson claimed that she "would not for worlds have them know that it troubled me" (L 175). Negative experiences such as these perhaps became the impetus for Dickinson's gradual withdrawal from formal worship services to her beloved home and garden where she could worship God more naturally and freely, thoughts she expresses in Poem 324:

Some keep the Sabbath going to Church —
I keep it, staying at Home —
With a Bobolink for a Chorister —
And an Orchard, for a Dome —

Some keep the Sabbath in Surplice —
I just wear my Wings —
And instead of tolling the Bell, for Church,
Our little Sexton — sings.

God preaches, a noted Clergyman —
And the sermon is never long,
So instead of getting to Heaven, at last —
I'm going, all along.

The universally popular hymn "All Things Bright and Beautiful" could not be a more appropriate companion to this poem. The buoyant theme of this hymn expresses a worshipful attitude toward God, the Creator of all Nature, a theme Dickinson conveys in the poem she called "My Sabbath." Using but slight liberty with the meter in the first stanza, which is also the refrain, the poem and hymn seem almost perfectly blended. Cecil Frances Alexander (1818–1895) wrote the words to this hymn and published them in her *Hymns for Little Children*, 1848. The hymn tune is Royal Oak, which is based on a 17th century English melody, which has an uncommon meter (7.6.7.6.) with refrain.

Another exultant poem is "Musicians Wrestle Everywhere," entitled "Melodies Unheard" by the editors when it was published in *Poems, Second Series* in 1891. This title could not be more misleading, however, for the poet is writing about music she *hears*. Indeed, she is engulfed within "crowded air" which is filled with the "silver strife" of wrestling musicians producing celestial music. Dickinson's acquaintance with the ancient myth of the "music of the spheres" as representing the sounds of heavenly perfection seems evident here. Up through the Renaissance and even later, the harmony of the parts of the cosmos and of the parts of the human psyche were seen as the basic elements of the same universal order, and Dickinson expresses the oneness of that universal order in this poem by attempting to describe an experience which defies human analogy. The music of the

ALL THINGS BRIGHT AND BEAUTIFUL

spheres, a central image in Christian musical thought, becomes the most adequate means possible to describe the heavenly music which the poet experiences in surround sound.

Such a revelation could not occur for Dickinson in a "dark, chilly, restricted church" which Mabel Todd earlier described, for to hear such music one must become a part of nature. Henry David Thoreau understood that concept, saying, "My profession is always to be alert, to find God in nature, to know God's lurking places, to attend all the oratorios and the operas in nature." Surely this was one of Dickinson's objectives as well.

The ebullient mood of this poem is profoundly evident in the lines "The 'Morning Stars' the Treble led / On Time's first Afternoon!" Dickinson's biblical knowledge provides the setting for this thought which is taken from the book of Job. In this particular passage, God is asking Job where *he* was when God laid the foundation of the earth, a period Dickinson terms "Time's first Afternoon." On this occasion, the biblical passage records, "the morning stars sang together, / and all the sons of God shouted for joy" (Job 38:7). In Poem 157, Dickinson expresses the same elation, which becomes a paean, a song of joy, incorporating Dickinson's love of music, of biblical knowledge, and of nature.

> Musicians wrestle everywhere —
> All day — among the crowded air
> I hear the silver strife —
> And — waking — long before the morn —
> Such transport breaks upon the town
> I think it that "New Life"!
>
> It is not Bird — it has no nest —
> Nor "Band" — in brass and scarlet — drest —
> Nor Tamborin — nor Man —
> It is not Hymn from pulpit read —
> The "Morning Stars" the Treble led
> On Time's first Afternoon!
>
> Some — say — it is "the Spheres" — at play!
> Some say that bright Majority
> Of vanished Dames — and Men!
> Some — think it service in the place
> Where we — with late — celestial face —
> Please God — shall Ascertain!

One wonders if this Dickinson poem became the inspiration for the popular hymn "This Is My Father's World," based on a poem written by Maltbie D. Babcock in 1901. These first two lines from the hymn would seem to indicate it was: "This is my Father's world / And to my listening ears / All nature sings, and round me rings / The

O God, Regard My Humble Plea

music of the spheres." At the very least, the emotional and spiritual response to nature expressed by both poets is similar and worthy of comparison.

The lyric strains of "Musicians Wrestle Everywhere" make it immensely suited for a musical setting, and a perfect match is found in an old hymn, "O God, Regard My Humble Plea," based on Psalm 61 and found in *The Psalter.* Lowell Mason composed the music in 1839 to the Meribah tune, which has a special meter (8.8.6.D).

The final poem to express jubilance is "Better — than Music! For I — who heard it —," a poem remarkable for its musical imagery. It was not included in the earlier editions of Dickinson's poetry, for Mabel Todd ceased publication of Emily's poems after a lengthy and highly unpleasant legal battle with Lavinia Dickinson over a piece of property both of them claimed. This poem, and many others now considered to be among Dickinson's best, rested in the camphor box where Todd had placed them until her daughter Millicent Todd Bingham, encouraged by her mother, brought all the remaining unpublished poems to the public in 1945 in the collection *Bolts of Melody*.

"Better — than Music!" describes an epiphany wherein the poet's heightened spiritual sensitivity allows her to hear celestial music which is beyond earthly description. So unique is this new music that comparison is futile and can only be partially achieved by relating it to what it is *not*. Dickinson's use of the word *translation*, as it was used in the King James Version of the Bible which Emily read, conveys a movement beyond the natural world. This movement beyond the temporal world pervades the poem and carries the poet into realms previously unknown, creating a spiritual euphoria.

In order to emphasize the magnitude of this elation, Dickinson contrasts it to the non-experiential "antique" biblical accounts, which are "Grandame's story," handed down from previous generations. Though she does not negate these ancient stories, they pale in comparison to the scintillation of her personal revelation. She longs to retain the freshness of the experience and desires "not to spill — its smallest cadence" but to hum this ethereal melody "for promise — when alone —," continuing to hum it until her "faint Rehearsal — / Drop into tune — around the Throne —." Perhaps Dickinson is recreating a scene from Revelation, her favorite book of the Bible, where the twenty-four elders fall down before God, and "cast their crowns before the throne, singing" (Revelation 4:10). Though the music is not heard by others, Dickinson absorbs the supernal sounds of heavenly melodies, and Poem 503 expresses her heightened spiritual awareness to its ultimate degree:

> Better — than Music! For I — who heard it —
> I was used — to the Birds — before —
> This — was different — 'Twas Translation —
> Of all tunes I knew — and more —
>
> 'Twasn't contained — like other stanza —
> No one could play it — the second time —
> But the Composer — perfect Mozart —
> Perish with him — that Keyless Rhyme!

COME, THOU LONG-EXPECTED JESUS

So — Children — told how Brooks in Eden —
Bubbled a better — Melody —
Quaintly infer — Eve's great surrender —
Urging the feet — that would — not — fly —

Children — matured — are wiser — mostly —
Eden — a legend — dimly told —
Eve — and the Anguish — Grandame's story —
But — as telling a tune — I heard —

Not such a strain — the Church — baptizes —
When the last Saint — goes up the Aisles —
Not such a stanza splits the silence —
When the Redemption strikes her Bells —

Let me not spill — its smallest cadence —
Humming — for promise — when alone —
Humming — until my faint Rehearsal —
Drop into tune — around the Throne —

A hymn tune to accompany this splendid poem might appear to be an impossibility, yet an Advent hymn, "Come, Thou Long-expected Jesus" so perfectly matches the meter of the poem that it would seem Dickinson had this very hymn in mind when she composed the poem. Charles Wesley wrote the words to the hymn, and it was published in *Hymns for the Nativity of Our Lord, 1744*. Rowland Hugh Prichard composed the music in 1830 to the hymn tune Hyfrydol, which is an unusual musical meter (8.7.8.7.D).

Countless other examples could be introduced to exemplify Dickinson's metrical proficiency, but these chosen poem and hymn combinations indicate the extent to which metrical hymn tunes were in her head during the creative process of writing her poetry. Samuel Barrows, a nineteenth-century critic, acknowledged Dickinson's creativity when he described her as a soul who "saw God, nature, and man at first hand, and made its own interpretation, its own alphabet and character," from which, he concluded, she "wrote her own hymnbook and her own ritual."[8] Dickinson was highly innovative when she chose to mold her profound poetic thoughts into the humble hymn form. By doing so, she discovered the capability of new effects on an existing meter, but even more so, she showed how successfully the hymn form could be utilized as an instrument to say something important and to create a totally new composition.

CHAPTER VI

Musical Settings
of Dickinson's Poetry

Four major aspects of Emily Dickinson's relationship to music have been established thus far. Chapter II concentrated on the musical imagery through which Dickinson expressed her profound thoughts and emotional moods. Chapter III discussed nineteenth-century recognition of the musical qualities of Dickinson's verse, while Chapter IV confirmed that Dickinson's poetic form was a musical one, based primarily on Isaac Watts's hymn-tune. Chapter V provided insight into the process of Dickinson's compositional techniques by indicating selected hymns which might have influenced her. All of these aspects combine to create polyphonic music which modulates through the major and minor keys of Dickinson's verse. Prominent as these musical attributes are to the integrity of Dickinson's lyric expression, my inspection of relevant materials revealed that no sustained literary commentary had yet focused on the total impact of this dynamic dimension in Dickinson's works.

It was at this point, however, that I discovered Carlton Lowenberg's book *Musicians Wrestle Everywhere: Emily Dickinson and Music.*[1] Dismayed and somewhat disheartened that someone had already published the discourse that I was attempting to complete, I read Lowenberg's book and found, much to my delight, that his study conflicted in no way with mine but rather provided the potential for an extremely important and innovative extension to my work. Whereas I had focused primarily on the musical qualities of Dickinson's poems and letters, one of Lowenberg's chief concerns was to provide bibliographic material on musicians who have responded to those musical qualities of Dickinson's lyrics by setting her poems to music. His study opened up the opportunity to combine literary and musical perspectives in order to create interdisciplinary insights into this important facet of Dickinson's verse. Therefore, in this chapter, my attention moves away from the effective means by which Dickinson achieved the musicality of her verse to the affective power of Dickinson's poetry as the primary motivational factor for the composition of numerous musical settings based on her poems.

Lowenberg's book provides an inventory of over 1,615 musical settings of 654 of Dickinson's poems and letters by 276 composers. Since the publication of his book in 1992, many additional musical settings of Dickinson's verse have been completed. From Etta Parker's setting of "Have You Got a Brook in Your Little Heart" in 1896 to the present, the number of musical settings has risen to nearly 3,000, with many more settings in the process of composition. To a remarkable extent, contemporary composers in ever-growing numbers are responding to Dickinson's poetry in a variety of ways as they transpose her melodic strains into musical settings which range from works for solo voice and piano to operas, choral works, and instrumental ensembles. Beyond question, these factors open up a completely new venue for the assessment of both the musical quality of Dickinson's verse and the musical responses to it.

The dilemma which Lowenberg's revelations presented was both enticing and frustrating. How indeed could this wealth of primary material be incorporated into my analysis of Emily Dickinson and music, an investigation which was nearing completion? But, incorporated it must be, for it soon became evident that musical interpretations of Dickinson's poetry are quite as legitimate as literary ones. Indeed, considering the recognized relationship that exists between music and poetry, the insights of musicians into Dickinson's poetry provide some of the finest and most perceptive analysis available.

With so many contemporary composers, most having composed numerous settings for a wide variety of Dickinson's poems, how could one begin to tap these vital resources in order to gain the most meaningful results? It soon became apparent that the focus should include only those American composers who had selected Dickinson's poems which contain musical terminology, thus layering the research already presented in Chapter II on musical imagery in Emily Dickinson's poetry. After narrowing the list to suit these criteria, I wrote letters to eighty-two composers and arrangers and received cordial and thoughtful replies from forty-one of them. I also received three telephone calls from composers who were interested in my research.

An overview of the contents of my letter to these musicians should clarify their responses to me and validate the extent to which their answers provide authenticity to this examination of Emily Dickinson and music. In general, after stating the purpose of my letter, I expressed delight that they and so many other composers had recognized the musical qualities inherent in Dickinson's verse. I suggested that the inclusion of pertinent comments from composers and arrangers about the creative interpretation of Dickinson's verse into the musical medium would add immeasurably to the depth and scope of my work. After explaining that one major section of my book was devoted to the Dickinson poems and letters which contain musical terminology, I identified their larger musical setting and then asked pertinent, succinct questions about certain appropriate poems within that setting. For example, I asked for their comments about the selection of these specific poems, their interpretation of them, and their attitude toward the texts of the poems as a whole. Also, I asked if the musical terms within the text had special meaning to them or received particular treatment in their setting. I assured them that such comments would assist me in providing an interdisciplinary approach to Dickinson's canon for those who tend to study her works solely from a literary viewpoint.

I was totally unprepared for the response which followed this letter. Not only did I receive contemplative and meaningful replies to my questions, I received abundantly more. Twenty-two composers and arrangers sent important, primary source material to me which I could not have obtained otherwise, and it seems appropriate to list those materials, for they suggest the intensity of the composers' involvement with Dickinson's poetry and its musicality, surely an important register of their critical responses. For instance, Gordon Getty sent a compact disc of *The White Election*, his song cycle based on poems by Emily Dickinson, and Robert Train Adams sent his CD of Dickinson songs, *Oure Pleasure*, plus manuscripts of eight of his Dickinson settings included on the disc. Sharon Davis sent her LP stereo recording which contains "Three Moods of Emily Dickinson," for which she was both composer and pianist. The following three composers sent tapes of their compositions: James Waters's *Goal*, a cycle of three Dickinson songs; Lee Hoiby's *The Shining Place*, containing five Dickinson songs; and Gerald Ginsburg's *All I Have to Bring*, plus the program notes and his manuscript music for five musical settings included in this tape.

Four other composers included manuscripts of their music with their letters. Jay Rizzetto sent "There's a Certain Slant of Light," and Tom Rasely sent two compositions of "Hope is the Thing with Feathers"—one by his father, Charles W. Rasely and one by himself. Roy B. Hinkle provided a manuscript of his composition, "A Service of Song," T.W. Higginson's title for "Some Keep the Sabbath." In addition to detailed information about each of her settings of poems with musical imagery, Margaret Foss Wood provided single manuscript copies of her music from *Opus 8 Harmony*, a compilation of sixteen poems by Emily Dickinson in musical settings.

Two arrangers with special interest in Emily Dickinson and hymns mailed large packets to me. One, the earlier cited Noel Tipton, sent an article he had written entitled "Hymns and Emily Dickinson." He also included the complete script of *Amherst Sabbath*, a play he has written with the encouragement of William Luce, author of *The Belle of Amherst*, and Dr. David Porter, a Dickinson scholar. In addition, he sent a tape of five of the hymn-songs for *Amherst Sabbath* along with copies of hymns he used in his play with poem titles which matched the meter and tunes of the hymns. John Gould, who uses Dickinson's poems set to hymn-tunes in order to teach poetic meter to his students, sent a copy of his essay "[Emily] Dickinsinging and the Art Thereof," along with the music for the hymn "The Church's One Foundation," to which he set Dickinson's poem "The Red Blaze in the Morning."

Others were generous with manuscripts and materials from

deceased family members, and these are of extreme importance in providing valuable primary source material which simply would not be available without their generosity. Otto Luening's widow, Catherine, sent me a copy of his biographical essay, "A Winding Path to Emily Dickinson," a work which provides keen insights into Luening's developing passion for Dickinson. Tom Leich, Roland Leich's son, sent the manuscript, "Setting Emily Dickinson's Poetry to Music," which are the notes for a talk his father gave at the College Club in Pittsburgh, Pennsylvania, on April 25, 1985. Tom Leich also provided me with seven individual musical pieces and two bound copies of Roland Leich's compositions, Volumes One and Five of *47 Emily Dickinson Songs*.

The families of two of the best-known composers of Dickinson settings, Ernst Bacon and Arthur Farwell, have been extremely generous in providing a considerable number of materials which would be totally inaccessible to me otherwise. For example, Ellen Bacon, widow of Ernst Bacon, sent a tape with excerpts of interviews her husband had given on Emily Dickinson. She also included some essays he wrote about Dickinson, plus a treasure trove of newspaper articles which have been written about Ernst Bacon's settings of Dickinson's poems.

Two of Arthur Farwell's children have shared valuable material with me, but they have provided a great deal more than that, offering insights into their father's passion for Emily Dickinson's poetry which resulted in his extraordinary output of musical settings of her poems. Brice Farwell sent his father's essay on Dickinson and material from Arthur Farwell's writings on Intuition, which explains in part Farwell's mystical relationship with Dickinson. He also included singer Paul Sperry's introduction to the Farwell Dickinson songs. Sara Farwell, Arthur Farwell's daughter, sent a five page, hand-written letter, beautifully expressing her recollections of the affinity her father had for Emily Dickinson and of his passionate dedication to setting her poetry to music.

Many additional composers, well-known and distinguished in their own right, answered my letters and provided primary source materials for analyzing musical settings of Dickinson's poetry. The plethora of replies created its own kind of problem, and that was how best to arrange materials which at times were similar and at other times diverse. First of all, it seemed desirable to quote the particular poem under discussion in its entirety. Following that, composers who have written musical settings for that poem discuss their individual responses, compositional processes, and musical interpretations. These narratives of explanation are, in fact, veritable anatomies of compositions, for they provide a rare opportunity to witness the minds of composers meeting the mind of the poet to form a new, joint creation.

Other studies on musical settings of Emily Dickinson's poetry have been conducted previously. However, these approaches are quite different from the one pursued in this chapter. For instance, works such as Jo Ann Margaret Sims's doctoral thesis, "Capturing the Essence of the Poet: A Study and Performance of Selected Musical Settings for Solo Voice and Piano of the Poetry of Emily Dickinson," and Inez Wager's article, "Emily Dickinson's Poems in Musical Settings," seek to identify the particular compositional devices with which composers have endeavored to capture various aspects of Dickinson's poetry.[2] Informative and instructive as these studies are, they differ from mine in that they rely mainly on secondary observation and study of the musical settings for their interpretations. Conversely, my focus is on the composers themselves as they provide interpretations of their musical settings in their own words and thoughts. This chapter is not designed to impose further interpretations on the musical settings other than what the composers themselves provide. To intrude on such primary source material would be both presumptuous and superfluous. Wherever comparisons and contrasts can be drawn among the various settings, commentary and analysis is provided. However, unless indicated otherwise, the composers speak for themselves. The message they bring provides a fresh approach and a unique opportunity to observe and appreciate the music of Emily Dickinson's poetry.

No attempt has been made in this chapter to place the poems and musical settings into categories, such as the familiar "Flood" subjects of Nature, Life, Death, and Immortality, for quite often a poem will encompass all of these subjects simultaneously. Instead, the poems and their settings are placed according to the *mood* of the poem, relying on the notion which has developed through the centuries that a poem or a musical work itself can be characterized as having a *mood*, for instance, of "inexplicable, yet inherent, suggestions of brightness or joy in the major mood and of pain or darkness in the minor."[3] Emily Dickinson herself wrote, "In adequate Music there is a Major and a Minor —" (L 370). The poems in this study fall quite naturally into one or the other of these two moods, for they exemplify "the shifts in mood and tone in Dickinson's poems, from ecstasy to despair, from a sense of the mastery of life to complete helplessness which characterized her writing."[4] The evocation of mood and emotion, an indispensable prerequisite in a poem to be used as a text for a vocal setting, is particularly powerful in Dickinson's verse, according to Jo Ann Margaret Sims.[5] For the most part, composers have matched Dickinson's moods in their musical interpretations of her poems, thereby bridging the gulf between the genres of poetry and music. Therefore, the purpose of this chapter is to elucidate the transmission of Dickinson's poetical expression of mood and emotion into musical expressions of infinite depth and variety.

What explains this exceptional affinity which composers have for Emily Dickinson? Perhaps composer Robert Starer has provided some of the most insightful reasons in this statement:

> Emily Dickinson's poetry is extraordinarily musical, so attractive to the musician's ear I am not surprised so many composers have set it to music. In her poetry every sentence is filled with meaning, every word is precisely right, her imagery is suitable to musical setting, and, above all, the rhythm of her language is so musical.[6]

Starer's conviction is echoed by many other composers. For instance, Kenneth Haxton states that Emily Dickinson is a poet whose work "is perfect for musical treatment," and Richard Hoyt declares that Emily Dickinson's poems "have so much music in them that it's hard to refrain from adding a few notes in way of a frame." Gerald Ginsburg claims that he loves to set Dickinson because her poetry is "the richest possible in imagery to spur the imagination of a composer and singer." In summary, Ernst Bacon, whose catalogue of Dickinson settings is considered one of the finest, wrote to opera singer Marian Anderson in 1939 that Emily Dickinson's "style of lyricism lends itself more perhaps than any other poetry of this country to musical setting, for it gives lyric expression to philosophical human thought without the latter being too apparent."[7] These comments, and many others which could be given, indicate that Emily Dickinson is the apparent poet of choice among contemporary American composers. According to their own acknowledgments, the composers included in this chapter have been borne up on a tide of genuine inspiration when setting Dickinson's poems to music, and, in many cases, they claim that the music has almost seemed to write itself. Whatever their particular biases and genres of music, these composers in general agree that much of Dickinson's poetry is pure music and her work is perfect for musical treatment.

The first serious composer to set Dickinson's poetry to music was Arthur Farwell, and for that he deserves special recognition in this chapter. Beginning in 1907 with "Sea of Sunset," he continued writing musical settings for Dickinson's poetry through 1947, setting forty of her poems to music in thirty-nine songs. Farwell's musical output was prolific, and a seventeen page catalogue of his works includes pieces in almost every form, from massive choral and orchestral works to solo piano pieces and songs, yet the musical works for which he may be most recognized today are his impressive settings of Dickinson's poems. Evelyn Davis Culbertson's comprehensive biography of Farwell, *He Heard America Singing: Arthur Farwell, Composer and Crusading Music Editor*,[8] details his status as a composer in the forefront of nearly every facet of the nation's musical life. Yet, a letter from his son Brice relates that Farwell told his children in his last years that he had begun to feel that "it was perhaps his Dickinson songs which he believed were the best expression of what he really wanted to say to the world with his music, of all the things he had composed." Farwell also shared with his children that Dickinson's "spiritual insight was a most vital aspect of his bonding with her nature."

Farwell's Dickinson settings had remained in relative obscurity until they were discovered by concert singer Paul Sperry, whose conviction that they were among "the very finest American songs" brought audience enthusiasm and wide acclaim to Farwell's works. Brice Farwell writes of hearing Sperry's concert of some of his father's Dickinson settings on the grounds of the Homestead in Amherst, Massachusetts. At that time Sperry remarked to Brice Farwell about how keenly Arthur Farwell "evoked the spirit of the verses in his set-tings and their accompanying piano treatments. Marty Katz, his pianist, agreed."[9]

Sara Farwell, Arthur Farwell's daughter and a professional actress, has performed as Emily Dickinson in *The Belle of Amherst*, a play based on the life of Emily Dickinson by William Luce, with music by Arthur Farwell. Sara Farwell shared some important insights about Emily Dickinson as a major influence on her father's musical output in a per-sonal letter to me. She tells of the great compositional output Farwell experienced under Dickinson's spell, a few pieces fairly early and then returning to her again and again when he was well into his seventies. In her opinion, each song was unique and individualized, as if her father had learned to play again. Farwell never talked at all about what happened to him when he sat down to write a composition, or explained an attitude or an approach that he might use in making the Dickinson settings, according to his daughter. Instead, she recalls, "I think by the time he wrote them, he was so familiar with the poems and somehow with *her* on every level and in every mode, that he no longer gave the usual thought to *how*,—he just *knew*." Of course, she states, he picked the poems that he had the deepest affinity for, and then "the right melody and key just sang in his head. They don't sound as if they came in bits and pieces, or by contrivance and juggling, but all of a piece." Sara Farwell writes that she imagines her father sim-ply being "bowled over" by discovering this incredible poet. She thinks it may have been years before he realized he "could and *must*" write his Emily Dickinson songs, and that then "it became one of the hap-piest collaborations of his life." In fact, Dickinson "waved a magic wand over the evolution of his own more and more original voice," she concluded.[10] Farwell, who often felt neglected and misunderstood by his contemporaries, would have been gratified to know that his own daughter understood him so well.

The only other composer to receive expanded recognition in this chapter on musical settings is the previously cited Ernst Bacon, who has been said to have "the largest and in many ways the best Dickin-son catalogue of all the composers."[11] Though his body of work includes symphonies, piano concertos, chamber music, ballets, and more than 250 art songs, as well as several books about music, his

Emily Dickinson settings have perhaps brought him his greatest renown, and he may well be her best interpreter. *A Singer's Guide to the American Art Song* records that Bacon's settings reveal he was "comfortable with the Amherst spinster's quirks and sensibilities," and somewhat amazingly, "his virile, forthright, expansive voice never overwhelms her delicate, cryptic, economic verse. What's more, these songs reveal him as a captivating melodist."

Bacon first came under Dickinson's spell in the 1920s, when he heard a lecture on her poetry in California. The impact on him was "immediate and significant."[12] In his essay, "On Words and Tones," Bacon described Dickinson as a lyricist with originality and inventive scope who could "compress immensity into four regular lines and with an economy as great as the classical Chinese poets and painters, conjure ecstasy, poignancy, immensity, grief, passion and intimacy with nature." Bacon musically matches this style in twenty-eight Dickinson songs recorded on the *Songs of Charles Ives & Ernst Bacon* disc. Though the songs cover a compositional period of more than thirty years, from 1931 to the 1960s, they remain consistent in that the songs are all quite short and concise, matching similar qualities in Dickinson's poetry. One critic, David Bradley, recognized this quality in Bacon's settings when he wrote in the *Journal of Singing*: "The gemlike, miniature feeling of each poem is captured well, with close attention to marrying the musical interplay of the texts to the actual music."[13]

Bacon found in the widely acclaimed concert singer Helen Boatwright the perfect solo voice to complement his Dickinson settings, and their concerts together received rave reviews. One review, for example, in the *Syracuse Post-Standard*, entitled "Emily Dickinson 'Returned to Life,'" praised these "two rare artists," proclaiming Boatwright to be that "consummate artist who knows exactly how to match the moods and images of the poetry with appropriate nuances and vocal coloration" while praising Bacon's composition as "lean and spare" to match Dickinson's verses, thus allowing "the voice with the telling words to shine forth in all their splendor." Praising Bacon's "mastery of the art of accompaniment" and Boatwright's "clarity of diction and expressive projection," the article contends that "a vivid third presence was evoked on the stage—the figure of the poetess herself."[14]

Reviews similar to this agree that Bacon's musical settings were highly successful in complementing Dickinson's poetry with added vitality. Perhaps Sara Hopkins has summed up Bacon's relationship with Dickinson best of all when she wrote the following:

> Bacon saw Dickinson as a vibrant human being, full of the passion, wit, philosophy, and sensitivity of all great poets. She was not strange or puzzling to him, and thus his songs flow from his natural appreciation of her intensity and lightness. Their freshness compares well to Dickinson's own.[15]

Certainly Arthur Farwell and Ernst Bacon deserve great credit for their intense, early interest in Emily Dickinson which resulted in outstanding contributions, both in quantity and in quality, to the catalogue of musical settings of her poetry. Yet there are many other outstanding composers who also deserve recognition for their passionate and creative musical responses to Dickinson's poetry. In the pages that follow, a number of these composers express the effect which Dickinson's poetry has had upon their lives and upon their musical settings of her verse. Unless otherwise stated, the words and thoughts which they express are their own.

Though the following composers respond to Dickinson's poems in various ways, Kenneth Haxton expresses the sentiments of many of them about the process involved in the selection of poetry for musical settings:

> The poems I choose for setting to music all meet certain criteria that I consider essential for good vocal texts. The words must be easy to comprehend when sung; the sense of the text must be easily understood, simple but not simplistic; there should be effective imagery; the sounds in the verse should be easy to vocalize—a preponderance of open vowel sounds; the structure of the verses must be interesting but not complex; and above all, the poetry must have a narrative drive or communicate strong emotion—preferably both. Surprisingly few poets meet these criteria. Emily Dickinson is a poet whose work is perfect for musical treatment.[16]

Examination of a number of Dickinson's poems and the musical treatment they have received from different composers provides an opportunity to see how poetry can inspire musicians and, conversely, how musicians can enhance poetry.

Five of the composers created musical settings for the following poem, "'Hope' is the thing with feathers" (P 254):

"Hope" is the thing with feathers —
That perches in the soul —
And sings the tune without the words —
And never stops — at all —

And sweetest — in the Gale — is heard —
And sore must be the storm —
That could abash the little Bird
That kept so many warm —

I've heard it in the chillest land —
And on the strangest Sea —
Yet, never, in Extremity,
It asked a crumb — of Me.

One of the composers to choose this poem is Robert Starer, who composed his setting "Hope is the Thing With Feathers" in 1977 for a four-part (Soprano, Alto, Tenor, and Bass—SATB) *a cappella* chorus. Starer says that he loved the poem's opening lines, particularly "That perches in the soul." The next line, "And sings the tune *without the words*" influenced his musical setting directly, he claims. Here, he has the tenors and baritones sing an *ostinato* melody on "Ah" while the sopranos and altos sing his setting of the Dickinson text above that. Later, the texture changes, he relates, but the "tune without the words" goes through the entire composition. Starer was also strongly impressed by the dramatic conclusion of the poem: "I've heard it in the chillest land." That, and the positive last line, "truly calls for musical treatment," according to Starer. [17]

This poem also served as inspiration for a musical setting by the late composer Charles W. Rasely, as well as for a setting composed by his son, Tom Rasely, who provided information about both of the settings. Charles Rasely's setting of "Hope" was started in May of 1969, at which time the composer claimed, "An opening phrase of the music occurred to me almost immediately. Then the remaining sections fell into place and came into being as an SSA (Soprano,

Second-Soprano and Alto) arrangement." Tom Rasely shared with me that his father's choral works were generally written for male and female parts (SATB) and that the decision to go with an all-female arrangement in this instance was singular. He believes that his father may have chosen the SSA voicing "to suit the lyrics—the fact that it was written by a female; the tenderness of the narrator's thoughts; the image of hope as a bird that sings sweetly; and 'never in extremity asked a crumb of me.'" These are not "guy" thoughts, according to Tom Rasely, and it would have to be agreed that they are not. Though Charles Rasely's female arrangement seems highly appropriate, "Hope" was eventually published in 1981 for unaccompanied SATB, primarily for marketing reasons.

Like Robert Starer, Charles Rasely was attracted to the phrase, "And sings the tune without the words." Rasely sets the melody over these words in a repeated pattern (G F# D E, G F# D E) and the figure is then mirrored at a lower pitch for "And never stops—at all" (D B G A B). Tom Rasely considers this "pattern writing" to be very typical of his father's writing: to establish a phrase, repeat it, and then do a recognizable variation on it. Tom believes that the combination of notes so close in range were probably meant to sound like a bird call. In so doing, he claims that his father would have been following the example of Beethoven and Mahler, two of his favorites.

When Tom Rasely examined his own setting of "Hope Is The Thing With Feathers," looking at it, he claimed, for the first time in over twenty years, he discovered that he was attempting to follow some of the compositional methods he had observed from his father. Tom's version, published in 1973, opens "with the notes cascading down from a repeated D note in the soprano." His intent, he said, was to have the sound "open up" like a bird's wings.

When Tom Rasely compared the two settings of "Hope," he found that his was "almost a mirror image" of his dad's setting of the opening line, "'Hope' is the thing with feathers —" for, he says, "We both left one note static while the other three voices move in parallel harmony (block chords). Interesting, don't you think?" Indeed it is interesting, and quite rare, to have the opportunity to observe father and son settings which seek to illustrate, in a musical sense, the ideas which Dickinson expressed in her poem.[18]

Composer Stanworth Beckler chose "'Hope' is the thing with feathers" as the second song in his *Five Poems of Emily Dickinson, Opus 56*, composed in 1961 for tenor, flute, bassoon, piano, and violin. Beckler, who claims that he and his wife have long been "in love with Emily Dickinson," considers "Hope" to be a fascinating vision, first, he finds, "as a piece of Emily's soul, and then as a flint from which we may strike our own sparks." He sets the tempo here as "marchlike, suggesting that 'hope' can go on and on, like an army marching ... somewhere ... which 'never stops at all.'"

Of the line "Sings the tune without the words," Beckler discerns that Dickinson obviously "prizes the tune," but he wonders if she feels herself "lacking in words." After all, he says, she never "drowns us in words; everything she says is sparse and trim." This Spartan aspect of her work is not particularly evident in his music, Beckler claims, except to the extent that his chamber setting avoids the richness and "redundancy of pitch" of an orchestral setting. He has rendered Dickinson more "pure and unadorned" here in this setting. At the very end of the poem, where Dickinson confesses that "never, in Extremity, / It asked a crumb of me," Beckler continues the march beyond the release of the voice on the word *me*, as a faint echo.

In this setting, Beckler has attempted to express the emotional content and the message of "'Hope' is the thing with feathers —." In doing so, he has accomplished the connection between poetry and music which he expresses in these words:

> All poetry worthy of being called "poetic" contains ingredients which can be discovered in a piece of music, an idea or "theme;" a structure within which the idea is manipulated, a presentation of the idea in which the emotional content and the "message" are expressed through changes of rhythm, pitch placement, and dynamics.[19]

Otto Luening is the final composer in my study to choose "'Hope' is the thing," which he included in his *Nine Songs to Poems of Emily Dickinson,* composed between 1942 and 1951. It is significant that the first performance of this work was given at the Vermont Composers Conference in Bennington, Vermont, in 1951, for Luening's intense interest in Emily Dickinson began at the 1940 Bennington Festival, where he attended Martha Graham's ballet production, *Letter to the World*, which takes its title from the poem by Emily Dickinson. In his autobiographical essay, *A Winding Path to Emily Dickinson*, Luening claimed, "Graham's production was a moving experience to me." He then read all the available Dickinson poems, selecting nine of them to set as a cycle for soprano and piano. For the cycle, Luening says, "I imagined mostly simple diatonic accompaniments, in themselves expressive. Emily's fine speech rhythms set the musical rhythms."

In his essay, Luening wrote that the line "'Hope' is the thing with feathers" suggested to him "a diatonic setting with important shifts from major to minor and the chord G, B flat, D, and F in the eighth measure, and the end of the song as a dramatic climax." Though the setting might recall a folk song, he claimed, the speech rhymes suggested an elastic tempo, as the sequence of the musical meter indicates (3/4 2/4 3/4 2/4 3/4 2/4 3/4 4/4 and later 5/4). Luening related that his song reaches a lyrical vocal climax at "That perches in the soul" and at "And never stops at all." For "And sore must be the storm — / That could abash the little Bird / That kept so many warm," Luening used a little rhythmic bounce before returning to the opening phrases. The final lines, "It asked a crumb of me," suggested to him the minor 7th chord on G of the opening. In the bass there is an allusion to Beethoven's *Fifth Symphony*. Luening, like the previous four composers of "'Hope' is the thing with feathers —" successfully conveyed the hopeful mood of Dickinson's poem in this musical setting.[20]

Composer Robert Train Adams's composition, *It Will Be Summer Eventually*, was composed in 1988 and is written for chorus, with variations between the male and female vocal parts to suit the text. His setting, which includes eight Dickinson poems, contains these three which are appropriate for my study: "It will be Summer — eventually," "The Robin is a Gabriel," and "I shall keep singing!" All of these poems, Adams says, were chosen as part of a larger set that "addressed the twin themes of the resurrection that comes as we move through spring toward summer, giving a view of the world from a New England vantage point." Adams claims that he was actually trying to create a work modeled loosely on Randall Thompson's *Frostiana*, with its mix of four-part choruses and men's and women's choruses, except that he wanted his to have a tighter structure. Adams states that he was attracted to Dickinson's work both because of her intense images and because of her punctuation, which freed him from the constraints of regular meter and presented interesting problems in developing a musical flow that would preserve the integrity of her writing while keeping the music moving.

For Adams, the text is all-important. He claims that it is the source of his musical material, and he finds that he spends much more time choosing text than he does writing music, partly because he first has to become immersed in the text. His general approach toward text interpretation is to try to get across the essence of the text as he feels or understands it. Sometimes he does word-painting if a particular word or phrase suggests itself. He did both in Dickinson's Poem 342, "It will be Summer — eventually," which follows:

> It will be Summer — eventually.
> Ladies — with parasols —
> Sauntering Gentlemen — with Canes —
> And little Girls — with Dolls —
>
> Will tint the pallid landscape —
> As 'twere a bright Bouquet —
> Tho' drifted deep, in Parian —
> The Village lies — today —
>
> The Lilacs — bending many a year —
> Will sway with purple load —
> The Bees — will not despise the tune —
> Their Forefathers — have hummed —
>
> The Wild Rose — redden in the Bog —
> The Aster — on the Hill
> Her everlasting fashion — set —
> And Covenant Gentians — frill —
>
> Till Summer folds her miracle —
> As Women — do — their Gown —
> Or Priests — adjust the Symbols —
> When Sacrament — is done —

In offering details of his composition, Adams refers first to the opening section which speaks of ladies, gentlemen, and little girls with dolls. He says it brought to mind a childhood taunt that kids used while playing: naa-na-na-na-naa-na. This taunt informs much of the melodic material. In measure 3 the high voices (soprano and tenor) mention the ladies, in measure 4 the low voices (alto and bass) mention the men. In measure 6, the little girls are portrayed by everybody, with a canon at the eighth-note to portray the bustle and jostling of children playing. This first section closes out with the opening two measures restated and extended to give the sense that "eventually" means eventually and not right now.

As the text continues to unfold, "bright Bouquet" is presented brightly and contrasts with the lower, slower, "drifted deep ..." which is followed by an extended "It will be summer" section. "The Lilacs" with their swaying are portrayed with changing meter, to give the effect of gentle moving with the breeze, while underneath "The Bees" move back and forth between two notes as if a simple tune is being hummed—followed by a reprise, greatly extended, of "It will be summer — eventually." The bog is lower than the hill; the Covenant Gentians have a couple of musical ornaments as frills. Concerning the ending, Adams explains, "As we approach the closing 'Sacrament,' the piece settles down to a chant-like mood, strengthening the connection between women doing their gowns and priests adjusting the symbols."

Word-painting is quite important in Adams's musical setting of the following poem, "The Robin is a Gabriel" (P 1483):

> The Robin is a Gabriel
> In humble circumstances —
> His Dress denotes him socially,
> Of Transport's Working Classes —
> He has the punctuality
> Of the New England Farmer —
> The same oblique integrity,
> A Vista vastly warmer —
>
> A small but sturdy Residence,
> A self denying Household,
> The Guests of Perspicacity
> Are all that cross his Threshold —
> As covert as a Fugitive,
> Cajoling Consternation
> By Ditties to the Enemy
> And Sylvan Punctuation —

Though this has fewer actual musical allusions than most of the poems in this chapter, Adams has created a musical setting which aptly describes the meaning of the poem. For instance, the line, "The punctuality of the New England Farmer" comes out in a certain stiffness and regularity in the lower voices. Adams has set the text to be sung only by women, to give the effect of the high-pitched voice of a bird. "As covert as a Fugitive, Cajoling Consternation" is set quietly with occasional louder outbursts to give the effect of the robin rather nervously telling an intruder to "get lost." Adams explains the spots like measures 32 and 36, where some of the voices stop singing in mid-word ("Punctua—" or "Punctu—" or "to the Ene—") or measure 33, where the choir stops in mid-phrase ("The Robin is a —") are intended to strengthen the sense of darting around, of "Cajoling Consternation." When speaking of "A small but sturdy Residence, A self denying Household," the lower two voices move homorhythmically in parallel fifths, providing a simple, spare structure, while the top voice provides a simple canon, yet a fifth higher, delayed by a quarter-note.

The third and final appropriate musical setting by Adams is based on the following poem, "I shall keep singing!" (P 250):

> I shall keep singing!
> Birds will pass me
> On their way to Yellower Climes —
> Each — with a Robin's expectation —
> I — with my Redbreast —
> And my Rhymes —
>
> Late — when I take my place in summer —
> But — I shall bring a fuller tune —
> Vespers — are sweeter than Matins — Signor —
> Morning — only the seed of Noon —

Adams chose this poem in part because of its musical terminology and in part because it referred to "a Robin's expectation," which suited the theme of his cycle. This text falls at the mid-point of his larger cycle, and it has the most complex texture: two choirs of three parts each. Adams explains that the two choirs work against each other, giving the effect of two birds, each trying to out-sing the other.

Later in "I shall keep singing" the text speaks of bringing "a fuller tune," at which point, Adams relates, "the two-choir counterpoint ceases and all six parts work together to be fuller." "Vespers are sweeter" is set more simply, with a chant-like flavor, so, he concludes, "the musical terms were very much a part of my thinking."

Adams contends that it is not so much that there is something musical about Dickinson's work, or that she uses musical terms, that makes it so easy and inviting to set to music, but that there's an integrity and richness of spirit in her work. He is attracted by the images she creates and the feelings she calls forth, and he responds to those images and feelings with his own images and feelings. Necessarily, he must surrender some of his artistic freedom because he cannot superimpose an arbitrary structure on a poem—at least not Dickinson's—but must try to discover what the poem wants to be. Adams claims that it is as much spiritual as it is intellectual. In summary, he says, "Perhaps that is why I enjoy setting Emily's poetry. My piece is not the poem, but represents, I hope, a collaboration between poet and musician."[21] Certainly, Robert Train Adams has successfully retained the light-hearted mood inherent in these three Dickinson poems as he has interpreted them musically in his settings.

Alice Parker is the only other composer to have three musical settings suited to the parameters of this chapter. Two of these poems, "I sing to use the Waiting" and "No ladder needs the bird but skies," are included in Parker's larger work, *Commentaries*, a cantata for two choruses of women's voices and full orchestra composed in 1978. The third poem, "One Joy of so much anguish" is included in *Echoes from the Hills. A Song Cycle on Seven Poems*. Parker expressed her attraction to Dickinson in these words: "I do love both her poetry and what I learn about it in attempting to set it. It's an inexhaustible source."

Parker opened her suite *Commentaries* with the following poem, "I sing to use the Waiting" (P 850):

> I sing to use the Waiting
> My Bonnet but to tie
> And shut the Door unto my House
> No more to do have I

> Till His best step approaching
> We journey to the Day
> And tell each other how We sung
> To Keep the Dark away.

Parker finds this poem to be a beautiful metaphor for life. She says, "Of course the poet sings—I'm convinced that lyric poems and songs come from the same part of the brain." Parker's setting conveys the idea that life is a journey—one ties one's Bonnet to prepare, and then wait for the approach of the Day, when we "tell each other how We sung"—the best method for keeping "the Dark away." Parker recognizes that "the enclosing of a cosmic idea within a tiny, structured form is typical of Emily's writing, as is the simple profundity of her language." Parker's setting captures the anticipatory mood of Dickinson's poem in a remarkable way.

The following poem, "No ladder needs the bird but skies" (P 1574), is included in Parker's *Commentaries*, which is based on five poems of Emily Dickinson and Southern folk-songs, hymns and spirituals:

> No ladder needs the bird but skies
> To situate its wings,
> Nor any leader's grim baton
> Arraigns it as it sings.
> The implements of bliss are few —
> As Jesus says of *Him*,
> "Come unto me" the moiety
> That wafts the cherubim.

Parker says that she loves the characterization of the conductor controlling his forces with a "grim baton"! And also the mental image of a choir of birds, dutifully obeying a tail-suited leader. Parker recognizes that Emily's extolling of the freedom of bird song—following its own immutable laws which are those of the natural world, and thus God's—stands in sharp contrast to the human model—as does the simplicity of the act itself, with no music books or rehearsal rooms.

From the light-hearted mood of the preceding two musical

settings, Parker creates a more somber mood for the Dickinson poem she included in her work, *Echoes from the Hills. A Song Cycle on Seven Poems*, which Parker composed in 1979 for soprano, flute, clarinet, horn, and string quartet. The poem, "One Joy of so much anguish" (Poem 1420) follows:

> One Joy of so much anguish
> Sweet nature has for me
> I shun it as I do Despair
> Or dear iniquity —
> Why Birds, a Summer morning
> Before the Quick of Day
> Should stab my ravished spirit
> With Dirks of Melody
> Is part of an inquiry
> That will receive reply
> When Flesh and Spirit sunder
> In Death's Immediately —

This poem has special meaning for Parker, who said, "This poem more than any other brings Emily to my mind's eye—the sleepless nights that she spent at her little desk, wrestling with huge thoughts undreamt of by her family—and what she must have felt, in the earliest dawn, when the birdsongs arose around her. The sweet joy mixed with her own anguish stood in stark contrast—as night and day, as human despair and natural rebirth." Parker considers "Dirks of melody" to be an unforgettable description of those brief phrases of song, as is Dickinson's final phrase: she will learn how all these opposites are reconciled when Death says "Immediately." Parker thinks it would have been so easy, and so proper, to say "In Death's immediacy," but she recognizes how much stronger Dickinson's image is. The affective power of Parker's musical setting is evident in the following account she shared with me: "I remember playing a tape of this song to a musical friend, and his wife coming in the room to listen. When I asked what had drawn her, she said she had to hear what all the birds were singing."[22]

Bird singing is an important part of "Some Keep the Sabbath" (P 324), which is the next poem in my study of musical settings:

Some keep the Sabbath going to Church —
I keep it, staying at Home —
With a Bobolink for a Chorister —
And an Orchard, for a Dome —

Some keep the Sabbath in Surplice —
I just wear my Wings —
And instead of tolling the Bell, for Church,
Our little Sexton — sings.

God preaches, a noted Clergyman —
And the sermon is never long,
So instead of getting to Heaven, at last —
I'm going, all along.

"Some keep the Sabbath" is one of the very few poems Dickinson named, and she called it "My Sabbath." Composer Roy B. Hinkle chose Colonel Higginson's title, "A Service of Song," for his musical setting which is included in his larger work, *On God, Love, and Nature*, which was composed between 1982-86 for high voice and piano. His setting, along with two other Dickinson settings, won him first place in a Composers' Competition in Reading, Pennsylvania in 1984. The judge of that competition stated that the songs illustrated a "sensitive marriage of words and music." In his musical interpretation of "A Service of Song," Hinkle endeavored to set the text in a playful manner because, in spite of being rather reclusive by nature, Emily Dickinson seems to have enjoyed her life and had fun in her own way, he believes. In the piano accompaniment for this song, therefore, he has employed running parallel intervals of thirds set as eighth notes to suggest Emily's naive playfulness.

In the sixth measure of the selection, as a setting for the words "I keep it staying at home," Hinkle has used a descending minor third intervalic drop in the melody which suggests a derisive melody strain that many children sing in a purposeful, or perhaps playful, mockery of their friends, for example, "Da-da-da-da-da-da—Sally's got a boyfriend." Hinkle adds that this descending minor third interval had been discovered by the composer-ethnomusicologist, Zoltan Kodaly, to be the interval sung by children at play universally throughout the world.

Another referential musical device Hinkle employed is a fast trill on the piano between C and D pitches. This trill effect is used in connection with the bobolink as a chorister in the wording "our little sexton sings." This leads to a *ritardando* effect in the music that results in Hinkle's introduction of the majestic tempo that accompanies in a chordal manner the words "God preaches" which is immediately followed by the more subtle volume side-response, "A noted clergyman." From there to the end of this rather short song, Hinkle uses the slower tempo until the closing accompaniment accelerates playfully in order to underline the optimism found in the last words of Emily's poetry—"I'm going all along."[23] It is clear that Hinkle successfully interprets the playful, optimistic mood of Dickinson's poem in his musical setting.

Composer Richard Hoyt created a musical setting for medium voice and piano of "Some keep the Sabbath," but he did not provide the extensive details of his composition as Hinkle did. Instead, he revealed some of his general compositional techniques. For instance, when he chooses a poem to set to music, he says that it is strictly a matter of the poem's magnetism at the moment. Musical terms are incidental to him; the overall mood and thought are determinant. Then he scans the poem and goes over the lines many times to find the musical rhythms he considers effective. After that, he says, "Melody evolves."

Hoyt uses a clanging-bell introduction in "Some keep the Sabbath" to hint of traditional keeping of the Sabbath. The accompaniment in this setting, as in his other settings, is invented to fit the mood of the poem. Hoyt concludes, "Emily Dickinson's poems have so much music in them that it's hard to refrain from adding a few notes in way of a frame. I am continually drawn back to her poetry."[24]

Composer Gerald Ginsburg "loves to set" Emily Dickinson's poetry which he believes is "the richest possible in imagery to spur the imagination of a composer and singer. She has written on every topic and her lines are pure music." Ginsburg's song cycle, *All I Have To Bring. A Cycle for Soprano and Piano* was composed in 1991, and Ginsburg considers it his best Dickinson setting. The cycle contains "Alabaster Chambers," based on the poem, "Safe in their Alabaster Chambers —" (P 216):

Safe in their Alabaster Chambers —
Untouched by Morning —
And untouched by Noon —
Lie the meek members of the Resurrection —
Rafter of Satin — and Roof of Stone!

Grand go the Years — in the Crescent — above them —
Worlds scoop their Arcs —
And Firmaments — row —
Diadems — drop — and Doges — surrender —
Soundless as dots — on a Disc of Snow —

Ginsburg claims that he was so in awe of this great poem that for a long time he was afraid to set it, until he realized one day that it's just a New England hymn, the kind of music Dickinson knew so well. Indeed, Dickinson called her poems "hymns," and Ginsburg discovered for himself that her poems were highly influenced by the structure and meter of hymns which she varied with her own sense of spontaneous rhythm. After that discovery, he reveals, the setting for this poem came easily. Ginsburg does not intellectualize when he is setting poetry to music, at least not consciously. Instead, he claims, "intellect merges with feeling and spirit. Dickinson's sublimity, for me, comes about because of her simplicity and natural awareness."[25]

Another poem which reflects on the passage of time with a mood of serenity is "New feet within my garden go" (P 99):

New feet within my garden go —
New fingers stir the sod —
A Troubadour upon the Elm
Betrays the solitude.

New children play upon the green —
New Weary sleep below —
And still the pensive Spring returns —
And still the punctual snow!

One of the outstanding characteristics of Dickinson's poetry, its ability to transmit mood and emotion, is beautifully demonstrated here. Composer Ronald C. Perera responded to these characteristics by including this poem in his larger work, *Five Summer Songs on Poems of Emily Dickinson,* which he composed for mezzo-soprano in 1969 and 1972. Perera's choice of these Dickinson poems was guided by the theme of nature in the seasons of spring and summer, and broadly speaking, the five poems are about the renewal of nature's bounty.

Perera says the fact that there is a musical allusion in "New feet within my garden go" is a happy artifact of his literary choice rather than being an integral part of his intention. Nonetheless, as a composer, he could not resist a bit of word-painting at the mention of the bird-troubadour. He gets a tiny four-note birdcall in the right hand of the piano accompaniment, a figure which occurs once more in the song at the line "and still the pensive spring returns." Apart from that, Perera claims that his setting is "rather gentle, rhythmically regular, and somewhat dark in character (perhaps the operative word is 'pensive' after all), as befits a poem about the cyclic character of winter and spring, life and death."[26]

A distinct mood shift occurs from the pensive one of "New feet within my garden go," to what composer David Irving terms the "remote and mystical" mood of the next poem, "There is a morn by men unseen" (P 24):

> There is a morn by men unseen —
> Whose maids upon remoter green
> Keep their Seraphic May —
> And all day long, with dance and game,
> And gambol I many never name —
> Employ their holiday.
>
> Here to light measure, move the feet
> Which walk no more the village street —
> Nor by the wood are found —
> Here are the birds that sought the sun
> When last year's distaff idle hung
> And summer's brows were bound.
>
> Ne'er saw I such a wondrous scene —
> Ne'er such a ring on such a green —
> Nor so serene array —
> As if the stars some summer night
> Should swing their cups of Chrysolite —
> And revel till the day —

Like thee to dance — like thee to sing —
People upon the mystic green —
I ask, each new May Morn.
I wait thy far, fantastic bells —
Announcing me in other dells —
Unto the different dawn!

"Cosmic dimensions and beauty of expression" are features of Dickinson's poetry that attracted David Irving to "There is a morn by men unseen," which he included in *Four Songs for Soprano, French Horn, and Piano,* composed in 1990. For Irving, this poem presents a vision of another world beyond the present, beyond life. He sought to compose his musical setting as a reflection of the eccentric and cosmic, for he found the mood of the poem to be "light, buoyant, yet profound, beautiful and mystical." Irving found the French horn to be ideal for evoking the mystery of a "remoter green" and "different dawn." The mood, he claims, had to be remote and mystical. Thus the harmonies he composed are employed in a manner that are reflective of the eccentric and mystical: major 7ths and bitonality produce the sense of remoteness, difference and the eccentric.

The only musical terms in this poem come in the words "dance" and "sing," and Irving says that they did receive special treatment in his setting. They come at the beginning of the fourth and final verse, and here, and only here, Irving makes a break with the strophic setting and writes new music for the phrase, "Like thee to dance, like thee to sing." However, the different treatment here has not so much to do with treatment of musical terms as it does with dramatic emphasis, for it asks in a dramatic and expressive manner: "Do you like to dance, Do you like to sing?" Breaking the strophic pattern here also serves to act as an announcement that the final verse has begun, Irving explains. He says that he has at times tried to reflect a musical term in a musical way in other songs, but he did not feel the urge or need to do so here, since the primary urge for him was to express the mood of this poem.

Irving contends, "With Emily Dickinson, her personality, her 'self' and her poetry coincide—they become the same, and that is what I wanted to try to convey in the music—not the sense of the reality of her or even her poetry, but the reality of *my* perception of her and her poetry. Thus it is the mood of the poem itself as well as the mood of Emily Dickinson herself, as I understand these to be, that I have tried to express."[27]

Emma Lou Diemer also composed a setting for "There is a morn by men unseen" which she included in *Three Poems of Emily Dickinson* for electronic tape in 1984. She considers this to be "an extremely musical poem, with references to dance, song, bells, movement," and she finds it to be "a hopeful poem though perhaps about death." She considers her electronic interpretation of this poem to be "vibrant, upbeat, and rhythmic."

Diemer set "There is a morn by men unseen" again in 1991, this time for chorus and orchestra, using the poem again for the reasons stated above. The setting, she says, is quite colorful and dramatic and is divided into several sections, corresponding to the verses of the poem. Diemer created considerable movement and rhythm for the first two verses. The third verse is set more quietly, very expressively, and is a soprano solo, with orchestral strings accompanying. Diemer found the last three lines of this verse "very imagist, very poignant, and the voice rises to high notes for 'the stars.' The last verse is set with some of the musical ideas from the first two: very rhythmic, building toward the climactic, repeated bell-sounds and hopefulness of the last few lines."

Diemer responded to the vivid imagery and musical qualities of another poem, "There came a Wind like a Bugle" (P 1593), which she also included in *Three Poems of Emily Dickinson:*

> There came a Wind like a Bugle —
> It quivered through the Grass
> And a Green Chill upon the Heat
> So ominous did pass
> We barred the Windows and the Doors
> As from an Emerald Ghost —
> The Doom's electric Moccasin
> That very instant passed —
> On a strange Mob of panting Trees
> And Fences fled away
> And Rivers where the Houses ran
> Those looked that lived — that Day —

The Bell within the steeple wild
The flying tidings told —
How much can come
And much can go,
And yet abide the World!

Diemer selected this poem for a set of electronic pieces that she composed in 1983 in quadraphonic sound, using synthesizer and computer. The poem, with the simile of a "bugle" and later the "bell in the steeple," suggested to Diemer "dramatic music, a bit brassy, bell-like, moving, dynamic." She believes that her electronic interpretation reflected this. Diemer says that she invariably chooses poems to set that have "an intriguing, colorful, imagist first line," and she contends that Emily Dickinson is "unsurpassed for this 'catchiness' of beginning," which is certainly evident in "There came a Wind like a Bugle."[28]

Lee Hoiby has also created a musical setting for "There came a Wind like a Bugle," and it is the fifth and final song in his larger work, *The Shining Place*, composed in 1954 for soprano and piano. He opens his composition with a proclamatory, trumpet-like motive, and he provides a rhythmic tolling in the accompaniment to indicate "The bell within the steeple wild." Hoiby finds that references to music in a poetic text, such as these, are always promising signs for him that they might make good songs. He considers this to be particularly true when, as is often the case with Dickinson, "the suggestion is that music and sound can convey a message or even an experience of the spirit in a more direct and public way than words can." Hoiby adds that "the reference to music in a song creates a useful point of cognitive overlap between the text and the setting, and a moment when the imitative 'mickey mousing' of textual imagery (which one usually tries to avoid) can be indulged in."[29]

In "There came a Wind like a Bugle," Dickinson focused on the destructive forces of the natural world, but in the following poem, "He fumbles at your Soul (P 315), her concern is on the destructive emotional power which is capable of scalping "your naked Soul":

He fumbles at your Soul
As Players at the Keys

Before they drop full Music on —
He stuns you by degrees —
Prepares your brittle Nature
For the Ethereal Blow
By fainter Hammers — further heard —
Then nearer — Then so slow
Your Breath has time to straighten —
Your Brain — to bubble Cool —
Deals — One — imperial — Thunderbolt —
That scalps your naked Soul —

When Winds take Forests in their Paws —
The Universe — is still —

Two composers chose this poem for musical settings. The first one, Carol Herman, included "He fumbles at your Soul" in her larger work, *Emily Dickinson: Four Poems for Soprano Voice & Bass Viola da Gamba*, which was composed between 1986 and 1991. Herman provided me with an unusually detailed description of her setting, and it is obvious from her details that she achieved a masterful blending of poetry, music and her musical instrument, the viola da gamba, in this composition, as the following comments will show.

This poem was suggested to Herman by Dr. Cristanne Miller (a noted Dickinson scholar and member of the English faculty at Pomona College), who invited Herman to perform her pieces at the International Dickinson Conference when it was held in Washington, D. C., several years ago. Herman decided "He fumbles" would be a most interesting poem to work on because it was about a subject she already knew intimately, and she found that the setting came together very quickly. Word-painting is something performers on historic instruments work with constantly, according to Herman, and she has given plenty of workshop classes entitled something like "Play the words with your bow." When she read "He fumbles," she was struck by what she felt would be a perfect marriage of Dickinson's words and what she could have the viol do. Herman's personal description of this "perfect marriage" is as follows:

> The piece starts with *pizzacato*—not bowed notes. This suggests the fumbling. The words "before they drop full music on" drops

in intervals for the voice; the viol does a chromatic scale—the "degrees." Under the words "prepares your brittle nature" the viol does *cal legno*, literally "on the wood," which is hitting the string with the bow wood—something often done in later music, but unusual for viols. Under the word "blow" the viol plays accented double stops which fade away dynamically under the words "fainter heard" and then *crescendo* again to the words "then nearer." There is a ritard under "then so slow." The viol then does a measure of agitated 16th notes and adds trills leading up to "your breath has time to straighten," during which the viol stops trilling and plays a long (straight) note. With "your brain to bubble cool" I used the rhythm of the words as spoken to copy for the viol rhythm.

The "imperial Thunderbolt" was great fun! I thought up the most dissonant chord I could manage to do on the viol. It is a really hard chord, and I even added fingering to help viol players. The soprano sings alone on "imperial Thunderbolt" and then the viol crashes in loudly with the chord. "Scalps your naked soul" is "naked" for solo voice in difficult, atonal intervals. The viol copies them an octave lower. There is a pause—then an entirely different idea for the last couplet. It is so gentle—so unusual. I remember working at it with some frustration, when all of a sudden the whole bit came together. The viol starts solo, and then repeats those measures while the voice comes in "gently and lovingly." The viol has a short solo bit and then gentle chords under "the universe is still." I gave the singer a VERY hard job for the last two notes—ending quietly with a high, octave leap. Under this the viol does something else unusual for the instrument—a harmonic. If done well, these hard last measures are, I think, most effective. But of course a lot of sopranos curse them!

This almost line-by-line analysis of Herman's composition provides an extraordinarily clear view of the process involved in one particular musical setting, and it indicates Herman's sincere desire to make her music reflect the text. In order to achieve this, Herman says that she would sit with her viol, read the words over and over, try to internalize their own rhythms, work on other interpretations, and experiment over and over again with what the voice and viol could do both separately and together to complement the words—and each other. Because the viol has the reputation of being close to the human voice, Herman says, "it is to me the perfect vehicle for working closely with words."[30]

Composer Paul Gibson composed his setting of the same poem for SATB a capella choir in 1988, and entitled it, "He Fumbles at Your Spirit." Gibson claims that as he searched for a text to set for unaccompanied choir, "the poem's striking imagery virtually jumped off the page with its power. Once I found that poem, of which I had never heard, I had no need to continue searching." The fact that the poem contains musical imagery was a bonus, not the primary reason, Gibson says, but that "bonus" was certainly a part of his response to the poem.

Gibson's first step, he relates, was to memorize and internalize the poem. He took it with him on walks and eventually, he says, "the basic melody had composed itself." Most of his work after that was to determine the exact harmony and voicing to convey the poem's power. From the beginning he knew that the music must be fairly simple and straightforward, to allow the words to be intelligible. Therefore, he planned on virtually no counterpoint or repetition. Though it is meant to be performed very slowly, the piece is still quite short, according to Gibson.

Gibson shared a comment he heard the evening that "He Fumbles" got its first recording. One of the baritones in the chorus asked him if this was a sacred work, and Gibson related that he was "taken aback." Up to that moment he had not considered the possibility, but he immediately saw that it was a completely valid approach. He added, "That this brief poem could have that richness, that either interpretation could be true, added to my appreciation of it and to my gratitude at discovering it." However, Gibson still prefers to think of "He Fumbles" as an intense reflection of the feelings we can undergo in love relationships of this world, and that is why it now concludes his new solo song cycle, *Strong as Death—Three Songs on Love.*[31]

"He fumbles at your Soul" was written in 1862, during a period when Emily Dickinson was undergoing a struggle of deep psychological dimensions. The last two poems under consideration were written around the same time, in 1861, and they also reflect the almost unbearable anguish which Dickinson undergoes as she experiences feelings of emptiness and loss of control. In the following poem, "I felt a Funeral, in my Brain" (P 280), Dickinson expresses an almost surrealistic mood of despair:

> I felt a Funeral, in my Brain,
> And Mourners to and fro
> Kept treading — treading — till it seemed
> That Sense was breaking through —
>
> And when they all were seated,
> A Service, like a Drum —
> Kept beating — beating — till I thought
> My Mind was going numb —
>
> And then I heard them lift a Box
> And creak across my Soul
> With those same Boots of Lead, again,
> Then Space — began to toll,
>
> As all the Heavens were a Bell,
> And Being, but an Ear,
> And I, and Silence, some strange Race
> Wrecked, solitary, here —
>
> And then a Plank in Reason, broke,
> And I dropped down, and down —
> And hit a World, at every plunge,
> And Finished knowing — then —

The strength of this poem lies in its consistent funeral imagery. Dickinson, through her poetic skill, takes a rational set of images and expands on them to describe mental states that are irrational. Three composers responded to these images and developed musical settings which reflect Dickinson's psychological state. One of these composers, Jules Langert, selected this poem for his larger work, *Three Emily Dickinson Songs*, which he composed in 1971 for voice and piano.

Langert relates that when he attempts setting a text of any kind, he tries to sense a mood or tone in the meaning and textual surface (mostly tempo, sound, the feeling of the stressed and unstressed words and syllables) to which he believes he can adapt a musical setting. In discussing the three Dickinson poems he set to music in 1971, Langert says that the first poem, "Pain has an element of blank" (P 650), and the third, "I felt a Funeral in my Brain," seem to share a contemplative anxiety and feeling of resignation. The second song, "To my quick ear the leaves conferred" (P 891), is more immediate and dramatic. Langert believes that in the context of the other two poems, "I felt a Funeral" is the recollection of a previously experienced state of mind; therefore it is less immediate, more reflective, and slower in tempo, like the memory of a dream. Langert set the first and third songs to be reflective and inward, with the middle song as a capricious and lively contrast.

"I felt a Funeral" is the slowest, most intense, and most expressive of the three partly, Langert says, "because of the especially rich imagery of the poem which most clearly suggests the disorientation of an obsessional or alienated state of mind." Langert set it as a kind of freely declamatory recitative accompanied by irregularly occurring chord clusters in the piano with the damper pedal held down almost throughout the song. Periodically, the soprano rises in pitch to a more or less anguished state of recall, and the first part of the song ends with the words "My mind was going numb."

Langert relates that in the final section of the song, a climax occurs on the words, "then space began to toll," in which the soprano sustains a low B, the lowest note of the song. Over this low note the piano begins a passage evolving from the chord clusters we have been hearing, into a clangorous solo which spans the full range of the keyboard. As it subsides, with the sound only gradually dissipating because of the held damper pedal, the soprano sings the final words of the poem accompanied by a few additional chord clusters. The only musical image Langert has specifically used in this setting is the "tolling" of space, like a "bell." He says that he thought of the drum image as contributing to the repetitive, nightmarish pattern in the poem, employed to heighten the general mood and intensity, but not urging him to use it as a specific musical reference.[32]

Kenneth Haxton also composed a musical setting for "I felt a Funeral in my Brain," and he included it in *Four American Women Poets*, written in 1984 for high voice and piano. Haxton chose "I felt a Funeral in my Brain," he said, "because it called out for a funeral march accompaniment, which, though an obvious solution, seemed appropriate to the poem and was a challenge." Unless the composer is careful, he added, marches can become imitative clichés. Haxton also found that the onomatopoeic repetitions "Kept treading, treading, " and "Kept beating, beating" certainly lend themselves to musical setting.

Emily Dickinson's meters are interesting to Haxton, and he finds them to be very "modern and elastic, avoiding the sing-song monotony of much of the poetry of that period." Obviously, according to Haxton, the well-constructed and balanced stanzas of most of Dickinson's poetry make it easy to construct melodies which can be repeated for emphasis. He says that in less formal verse forms motifs have to be used, both in the texts themselves and in the accompaniments. This is effective and unifying but is possibly not always as successful for the listener's ear as establishing a melodic line which can more easily be assimilated, Haxton argues.[33]

Composer James Waters included "I felt a Funeral in my Brain" in his musical setting entitled *Goal*, which he composed in 1982 for mezzo-soprano solo, percussion (4 timpani, marimba, orchestral bells [chimes], 2 tom-toms [low and high], 2 wood blocks), piano, viola, and violoncello. The other two songs in *Goal* are "One need not be a Chamber to be haunted" (P 670) and "I felt a Cleaving in my Mind" (P 937). Waters says that he chose all the poems of *Goal* in order to achieve his concept of the cycle as a whole, and all three songs express some of the "debilitating psychological states which can occur in life."

Waters considered "I felt a Funeral" to be a slow procession, and he set it with very slow, low beats which are almost, but not quite, even. At first these beats are performed only by hitting the strings of the piano, but drum-beats begin with the entrance of the drum at the beginning of the second stanza as a part of the building up of the processional. These beats become faster as the tension rises and cease with the line "As all the Heavens were a Bell," which he considers to be a mental space filled with bells. Waters has the tubular chimes playing a profusion of notes at this point, the climax of the poem, and even the piano imitates bells. The climax stops quickly, and Waters has made the last two lines almost bare—"silence" and "solitary" are the operative words.

Waters provided some insightful remarks about his compositional techniques. He explained that what he tries to do is to expand, by musical means, the "meaning" of the poem, very broadly interpreted. His intention in setting the poem is to express the intent of the poet, as he understands it. This process is less dependent on the denotative meaning of the words than on the form, poetic rhythm, and the pure sound of the spoken (sung) words. Sometimes he will try to make the music refer to one specific word, as he did with "bell," but this is less important to him than the totality of the piece which is based on the whole poem.[34]

Analysis of selected musical settings of Emily Dickinson's poems concludes in this chapter with one of Dickinson's best known poems, which is generally considered her finest poem on despair, "There's a certain Slant of light" (P 258):

> There's a certain Slant of light,
> Winter Afternoons —
> That oppresses, like the Heft
> Of Cathedral Tunes —
>
> Heavenly Hurt, it gives us —
> We can find no scar,
> But internal difference,
> Where the Meanings, are —
>
> None may teach it — Any —
> 'Tis the Seal Despair —
> An imperial affliction
> Sent us of the Air —
>
> When it comes, the Landscape listens —
> Shadows — hold their breath —
> When it goes, 'tis like the Distance
> On the look of Death —

Composer Sharon Davis includes "There's a certain Slant of light" in her larger work, *Three Moods of Emily Dickinson*, which she composed in 1976 for soprano, violin, cello, and piano. She chose this particular poem, Davis says, "because it expressed the same feeling I had on certain somber winter afternoons in my childhood—nothing extraordinary or earth-shaking—just a subtle touch of an unnamed bleakness or gloom." Overall, she has set this song so that it is somber and stark in order to project that same bleak feeling. The piece is built on a 12-tone row, and in the middle section the speaking voice (*sprech-stimme*) is used as a dramatic emphasis. Davis explains that during the measures when the soprano sings "cathedral tunes," the violin ascends, as does a vaulted ceiling, and the piano descends in fifths, as in later Gregorian chants. The title of this work as a whole refers to Dickinson's moods, according to Davis, who considers that these moods may indeed represent the poet's alter-egos.[35]

"There's a certain Slant of light" is one of the poems included in Jay Rizzetto's piece, *Five Poems of Emily Dickinson*, which he composed in 1978. His setting employs the solo trumpet as an illuminator of the text; that is, the trumpet interplays with the narrator. Rizzetto, in discussing his setting, relates that the piece starts with the trumpet playing "bell tones," a term brass players know to mean "bell-like." The tones are slow and strong; they introduce the narrator's line. When she or he comes in, the bell tones continue but as background in a piano dynamic. They are representative of cathedral sounds: Dickinson's "cathedral tunes." Also, Rizzetto adds, if you know New England winters, you understand what she means about "that slant of light" and its oppression, although her meaning goes deeper than winter's light. In short, according to the composer, "the music illuminates 'the seal despair,' and it is certainly the darkest musical setting of the five pieces.[36]

Dan Locklair's setting of "There's a certain Slant of light" is found in his 1982 *two soprano songs*, published by Subito and distributed by T. Presser. Long an admirer of Emily Dickinson's poetry, Locklair finds her poems "full of wonderful imagery, depth of feeling, distinctive personality and American." Locklair claims that Dickinson's poetry possesses a natural lyricism which, in one way, hardly makes it necessary to set the poems to music at all and yet, on the other hand, makes the poems so natural for a composer to set.

Though Locklair has great admiration for Dickinson's poetry, he has set only one of her poems. The circumstances surrounding this single exception occurred in 1982, when he was asked to consider creating a new vocal work based on a Dickinson poem for a planned Dickinson symposium to be held in December of that year at the

Reynolda House Museum of American Art in Winston-Salem, North Carolina. Of the poems submitted to Locklair (for which few if any vocal settings had been done), his favorite was "There's a certain Slant of light."

Locklair was attracted to the dualities of light and dark in the poem and sought to convey this in his vocal setting for soprano and piano. According to Locklair, he sought to use a quick, gentle, glistening, often high-register idea in the piano part to convey the sense of the "Slant of light." The darker elements of the poem, such as "Winter Afternoons," are conveyed "through a musical idea of heavy, dark, low-register, long-note F-sharp minor chords," Locklair explains. A third musical idea (a short, two-measure plainsong-like passage) reflects the "Cathedral Tunes" and is the lyrical idea on which the soprano's main material throughout the piece is built. In addition to it being a quality found in much of his writing for piano in general, the piano's sustain pedal is held down throughout the entire duration of the piece in order to give a dream-like quality to the entire Dickinson poem. Molding words to music so that the two form a perfect "marriage" is Locklair's goal in all of his musical settings, and he hopes that he has achieved that goal here.[37]

The final comments on "There's a certain Slant of light" come from Robert Baksa, who included this poem in his setting, *More Songs to Poems of Emily Dickinson*, which was composed in 1967 for soprano or mezzo-soprano and piano. Baksa says that in order for him to be interested in setting a poem it must have a certain mood. Here, in a few short lines, he believes that Dickinson superbly captures the feeling of desolation. Baksa finds that he can scarcely bring to mind a finer example of her genius.

Baksa begins his setting with eight measures of static harmony which portray the desolate tone of the verse. Each phrase of the poem is underscored by this static harmony. Baksa was struck by the opening line where Dickinson speaks of the "weight of cathedral tunes." This suggested broad organ-like chords. Yet the dissonant descending harmonies, he feels, keep the sound oppressive rather than grandiose. Each line of the text is followed by this solemn music which at the end fades away into utter despair under the words "'tis like the distance on the look of death." Among his settings of Dickinson's poetry, this is one of Baksa's favorites because he feels that he came close to truly "capturing" the poem. He concludes, "For me this means that not only is there music accompanying the words but that it amplifies and heightens what is already there in the poetry."[38]

Baksa has come very close to summing up the stated intent of all the composers included in this chapter. In their own words and thoughts, these composers have shared their attraction to Dickinson's poetry and their desire to capture the moods of her poetry in their musical settings. By their own admission, these contemporary composers seem to share an almost symbiotic relationship with the nineteenth-century poet. They have responded to Emily Dickinson's poetic moods, which range from the ebullience of "'Hope' is the thing with feathers" to the oppressiveness of "There's a certain Slant of light," by creating compositions that reflect these moods in music. In every instance, these composers have attempted to wed music to text in order to achieve a unity whereby one art form enhances the other. In this process, Dickinson's poetical moods have been interpreted and translated into their musical moods.[39]

In his essay, "On Words and Tones," Ernst Bacon wrote, "Words and tones are immemorially bound together, though neither can explain the other.... While words can evoke tones, there is no literary skill that can describe melody.... Musical composition, like poetry, cannot be taught." That was a concept Emily Dickinson understood, as she revealed in an early letter to Colonel Higginson, seeking his literary advice: "I would like to learn — Could you tell me how to grow — or is it unconveyed — like Melody — or Witchcraft?" (L 261). Though neither musical composition nor poetry can be taught, the spirit of inspiration behind these two art forms can unite to create a new medium of expression which magnifies the best in both.

CHAPTER VII

Musical Reflections on Dickinson's Poems and Letters

What explains the widespread and ever increasing popularity of Emily Dickinson's prose and poetry? What was present in her verse from the beginning that continues to attract world-wide attention to the Dickinson canon? Ever since Thomas Johnson published *The Complete Poems of Emily Dickinson* in 1955, scholars have been seeking to find explanations for the universal appeal of Dickinson's works. For instance, Jay Leyda's intent in his two-volume documentary, *The Years and Hours of Emily Dickinson,* is to get at the truth of Emily Dickinson. He believes that any fact, no matter how trivial, is important, for the tiniest scrap of biographical information may be the detail which reveals a major theme or continuity in the poems. Robert Weisbuch chooses to view Dickinson's lyrics as one long poem, to the same extent that Walt Whitman's lyrics constitute *Leaves of Grass.* Weisbuch's search has been for the underlying characteristics which unite the poems, isolating these characteristics with the hope of finally achieving an integration which will not compromise the poems' variety. And Barton Levi St. Armand, who studies Dickinson in her nineteenth-century culture, believes that every deep consideration of a work of art must develop an approach to that art that is interdisciplinary as well as unique. St. Armand suggests that Dickinson's art may be likened to that of a pieced quilt, and he proposes to examine the general fabric of the culture from which Dickinson cut her "blocks," refashioning them in her own unique way. By so doing, he hopes to find some common thread that will allow Dickinson's work to be viewed as an organic whole.

Music may well serve to fill the criteria set out by these three scholars, for it provides the continuity in both Dickinson's life and works which Leyda seeks; it serves as an underlying characteristic for Weisbuch's search; and it provides the common thread which St. Armand desires in order to view Dickinson's canon as an organic whole. In fact, Dickinson's poems and letters comprise a grand symphony in which music becomes a vibrant thread, weaving in and through Dickinson's major themes of Life, Death, Love, Nature, and Immortality.

Dickinson herself may have given us a clue about the importance of this connecting thread in an early letter she wrote to her friend Jane Humphrey describing her feelings about all that was taking place in her life: "... it's all wrong unless it has one gold thread in it, a long, big shining fibre which hides the others — and which will fade away into Heaven while you hold it, and from there come back to me." Then she asks Jane, "What do you weave from all these threads?" (L 35). Richard Sewall believes this metaphoric passage may well announce Dickinson's dedication to a life of poetry, and, for Dickinson, music serves as a metaphor for poetry. Music, then, may well be the "one gold thread" that interweaves, highlights, and connects her most important themes.

It is well known that Dickinson considered publication to be "the auction of the mind," yet she did not request the destruction of her poems following her death, perhaps anticipating that her poetry might later become her "letter to the world." It is not excessive to say that her 'letter" was also her "rhapsody," the root word of which means "one who strings songs together." That definition gains significance when related to Millicent Todd Bingham's initial reaction to some of Dickinson's poems which had been stored in a camphor box for a number of years. In her introduction to *Bolts of Melody*, Bingham describes her impression of these poems:

The arrangement, verse form, and in particular the punctuation were not clearly indicated. In some poems dashes are sprinkled so lavishly that they give to the page the appearance of a thread on which the phrases are strung.

Perhaps Bingham's mother, Mabel Loomis Todd, had recognized this same characteristic of Dickinson's poems when she transcribed them for publication, for in one of her lectures about Dickinson's poetry, Todd says, "Emily Dickinson's prophetic vision and uplift of soul were sublime, and her 'irresistible needle-touch' has pierced to the core of many of the deepest and finest things of life."[1] Certainly music is one of the "long, big shining fibres" which Dickinson's "irresistible needle-touch" transforms into the grand tapestry of her verse. Sometimes it is muted and dull, barely visible at all. At other times, the golden, melodic strand glistens brightly and becomes the focal point of the work.

There can be no doubt that music served Dickinson's creative purposes by enhancing and illuminating the lyrical setting in many of her verses. Dickinson's background in music provided her with rich musical metaphors, allusions, and imagery which add dimension to the depth and quality of her verse. The poet's life itself was filled with periods of harmony and periods of dissonance, and her profound poetical gift allowed her to interpret these periods, often in musical imagery, to reflect the major and minor keys of her life.

Musicians, in particular, have responded emotionally to Dickinson's various moods and have sought to interpret and transcribe them into the abstract language of music. In this process, they are seeking to convey the tone behind each poem they set. Composer Jules Langert expresses the feelings of many musicians when he says, "There is strong emotion in Dickinson's work, and also a great economy of language, which allows the musical setting wide scope."[2] In general, musicians attempt to highlight the text and never overshadow it, allowing Dickinson's poetic voice to sing through. Numerous composers have responded to the musical essence inherent in Dickinson's poetry, and they have placed her poems into musical settings which range from classical to rag-time to rock, indicating the vibrant, energetic, and flexible qualities of Dickinson's verse.

Perhaps these are some of the same qualities Dickinson implied in a letter to T.W. Higginson, seeking literary advice: "Are you too deeply occupied to say if my Verse is alive?" (L 260). Though F. O. Matthiessen was not responding to this question when he wrote the following statement, his insights could certainly be applied to Dickinson's verse and could not be more appropriate:

> For the verse is not a vehicle to carry a sentence as a jewel is carried in a case: the verse must be alive, and inseparable from its contents, as the soul of man inspires and directs the body, and we measure the inspiration by the music.[3]

The musical inspiration behind Dickinson's verse is at least a part of its cosmopolitan attraction, and her appropriation of the universal language of music as a key element in her verse adds immensely to her popular appeal. As Rita Aiello has noted, "Music and language are universal, innate expressions of human cognition and communication,"[4] a concept Dickinson expresses in this way: "The earth has many keys. / Where melody is not / Is the unknown peninsula." (P 1775).

Throughout her life, Dickinson found herself surrounded by the sounds of music. For her, "Musicians wrestle everywhere — / All day — among the crowded air / I hear the silver strife —" (P 157), and she reaches out into this musical atmosphere for notes, sometimes joyous and sometimes plaintive, to create variations in the theme song of her melodic verse. Dickinson observed, "In adequate Music there is a Major and a Minor" (L 370), and it is this same combination which gives variety and impact to Dickinson's poetry as she plays upon the emotions of her readers through her "songs."

Emily Dickinson considered herself a songbird, and no one recognized that fact better than her friend Mabel Loomis Todd, who significantly records that "bluebirds and orioles were singing ecstatically" when Emily Dickinson's funeral procession passed slowly through blossoming fields toward the family burial site.[5] Susan Dickinson, in her obituary for Emily, wrote that "Her swift poetic rapture was like the long glistening note of a bird one hears in the June woods at high noon, but can never see," adding that Dickinson "walked this life with the gentleness and reverence of old saints, with the firm step of martyrs who sing while they suffer."[6] The importance of music in Emily Dickinson's life and in her prose and poetry can not be over-stated, and her musical verse continues to "stun" the world "With Bolts of Melody!"

Notes

Preface

1. Thomas H. Johnson, ed., *The Complete Poems of Emily Dickinson,* (Cambridge, Mass.: The Belknap Press of Harvard University Press, 1979). Hereafter, Dickinson's poems are cited in the text by P and the Johnson number. I have retained the grammar, punctuation and spelling from the Johnson edition.

2. Thomas H. Johnson, ed., *The Letters of Emily Dickinson* (Cambridge, Mass.: The Belknap Press of Harvard University Press, 1986). Hereafter, Dickinson's letters are cited in the text by L and the Johnson and Ward number. I have retained the grammar, punctuation and spelling from the Johnson and Ward edition.

3. Poul Bondesen, *North American Bird Songs: A World of Music (Klampenborg:* Scandinavian Science Press, 1977) 26.

4. As quoted in Bondesen 26.

5. William Homan Thorpe, *Bird-Song: The Biology of Vocal Communication and Expression in Birds* (Cambridge: Cambridge University Press, 1961) 20.

6. Thorpe 5.

7. Richard B. Sewall, *The Life of Emily Dickinson* (New York: Farrar, Straus and Giroux, 1980) 261.

Chapter I. Musical Background of Dickinson's Life and Times

1. Charmenz S. Lenhart, *Musical Influence on American Poetry* (Athens: University of Georgia Press, 1956) 209.

2. Richard B. Sewall, *The Life of Emily Dickinson* (New York: Farrar, Straus and Giroux, 1980), 215.

3. Millicent Todd Bingham, *Ancestor's Brocades: The Literary Debut of Emily Dickinson* (New York: Harper, 1945) 12.

4. Sewall 218.

5. Jay Leyda, *The Years and Hours of Emily Dickinson*, 2 vols. (New Haven: Yale University Press, 1960) I: 86.

6. Leyda I: 367.

7. Leyda I: 301–302.

8. Millicent Todd Bingham, *Emily Dickinson's Home: The Early Years as Revealed in Family Correspondence and Reminiscences* (New York: Dover, 1967) 143.

9. Leyda II: 273.

10. Judy Jo Small, *Positive as Sound: Emily Dickinson's Rhyme* (Athens: University of Georgia Press, 1990) 70.

11. Sewall 11.

12. Barton Levi St. Armand, *Emily Dickinson and Her Culture: The Soul's Society* (Cambridge: Cambridge University Press, 1986) 15.

13. Jane Donahue Eberwein, *Dickinson: Strategies of Limitation* (Amherst: University of Massachusetts Press, 1985) 262.

Chapter II. Musical Imagery
in Dickinson's Poems and Letters

1. Thomas Carlyle, *On Heroes, Hero-Worship, and the Heroic in History* (Berkeley: University of California Press, 1993) 71–72.

2. This poem indicates Dickinson's prescience about music emanating from the grass, for, according to D'Olivet, "scientists have only recently learned that the particles of an oxygen atom vibrate in a major key and that blades of grass 'sing'." See Antoine Fabre D'Olivet, *Music Explained as Science and Art* (Rochester, VT: Inner Traditions, 1987) 185.

3. Richard B. Sewall, *The Life of Emily Dickinson* (New York: Farrar, Straus and Giroux, 1980) 270.

4. Charles R. Anderson, *Emily Dickinson: Stairway of Surprise* (New York: Holt, Rinehart and Winston, 1960) 200.

5. Jane Donahue Eberwein, *Dickinson: Strategies of Limitation* (Amherst: University of Massachusetts Press, 1985) 261.

6. Adrienne Rich, "Vesuvius at Home: The Power of Emily Dickinson," *Shakespeare's Sisters: Feminist Essays on Women Poets,* ed. by Sandra M. Gilbert and Susan Gubar (Bloomington: Indiana University Press, 1979) 114.

7. John Cody, *After Great Pain: The Inner Life of Emily Dickinson* (Cambridge: Belknap of Harvard University Press, 1971) 6.

Chapter III. Musical Qualities of Dickinson's Poetry: Nineteenth-Century Views

1. Richard B. Sewall, *The Life of Emily Dickinson* (New York: Farrar, Straus and Giroux, 1980) 170.
2. Willis J. Buckingham, ed., *Emily Dickinson's Reception in the 1890s: A Documentary History* (Pittsburgh: University of Pittsburgh Press, 1989) xi. Unless otherwise noted, the remaining notes for this chapter indicate the entry numbers corresponding to those which Buckingham has assigned to each document in this documentary work.
3. Buckingham xx.
4. Buckingham xiv.
5. #318. Unlocated clipping, December 20, 1891.
6. #287. *Truth*, ca. December 1891.
7. #515. "Books and Authors." *Boston Sunday Courier* 102 (September 6, 1896, [3].
8. #17. A. T. "An Edition of the Poems of Emily Dickinson." *Boston Daily Traveller,* November 22, 1890, II.
9. #581. A. von E. "For the Women's Section: Emily Dickinson, Part II." *Der Westen,* June 19, 1898, sect. 3, 1.
10. #553. [Rupert Hughes.] Chelifer (pseud.). "The Ideas of Emily Dickinson." *Godey's Magazine* 133 (November 1896), 541–43.
11. #126. Andrew Lang. "Some American Poets." *Illustrated London News* 98 (March 7, 1891), 307.
12. #64. (William Dean Howells.) "Editor's Study." *Harper's New Monthly Magazine* 82 (January 1891), 318–21.
13. #72. [Andrew Lang.] "The Newest Poet." *Daily News* [London], January 2, 1891, 5.
14. #145. [Samuel J. Barrows.] "Emily Dickinson's Poems." *Christian Register* 70 (April 30, 1891), 274.
15. #283. *Fall River* [Mass.] *Monitor,* ca. December 1891.
16. #27. [Robert Bridges.] Droch (pseud.). "Bookishness." *Life* 16 (November 27, 1890), 304.
17. #300. "Books and Bookmen." *Light* 4 (December 5, 1891), 322.
18. #16. "Books and Authors." *Boston Home Journal,* n.s. 4 (November 22, 1890), 10.
19. #83. "New Books." *Commonwealth* 30 (January 10, 1891), 8.
20. #13. [Charles Goodrich Whiting.] "The Literary Wayside." *Springfield Republican,* November 16, 1890, 4.
21. #28. [Thomas Wentworth Higginson.] "Recent Poetry." *Nation* 51 (November 27, 1890), 422–23.
22. #587. Bliss Carman. "Bliss Carman's Marginal Notes." *Chicago Post,* July 15, 1899, 7.

23. #310. "Today's Literature." *Chicago Tribune,* December 12, 1891, 12.

24. #543. [Thomas Wentworth Higginson.] "Recent Poetry." *Nation* 63 (October 8, 1896), 275.

25. #491. Mabel Loomis Todd. "Emily Dickinson's Letters." *Bachelor of Arts* I (May 1895), 39–66.

26. #480. "Out and About." *Worcester* [Mass.] *Spy,* January 24, 1895, 4.

27. #301. "Poems Fresh From the Press." *Cleveland Sunday Plain Dealer,* December 6, 1891, 4.

28. #21. [Arlo Bates.] "Books and Authors." *Boston Sunday Courier* 96 (November 23, 1890), 2.

29. #135. Mary D. Cutting. "Literature." *Christian Inquirer* 4 (April 9, 1891).

30. #343. *Concord* [N. H.] *People and Patriot,* February 1892.

31. #359. W. M. "Emily Dickinson's Poems." *Housekeeper's Weekly* 3 (April 9, 1892), 4.

32. #194. E. R. "Talk About Books." *Queen, The Lady's Newspaper* [London] 90 (August 15, 1891), 253.

33. #232. [Andrew Lang.] "An American Sappho." *London Daily News,* October 3, 1891, 4–5.

34. #545. "Emily Dickinson's Poems." *New York Commercial Advertiser,* October 10, 1896, 14.

35. #71. *Concord* [N. H.] *People and Patriot,* January 2, 1891.

Chapter IV. Musical Form of Dickinson's Poetry: Contemporary Perspectives

1. Thomas H. Johnson, *Emily Dickinson: An Interpretive Biography* (Cambridge: Harvard University Press, 1955) 84.

2. Martha Winburn England and John Sparrow, *Hymns Unbidden: Donne, Herbert, Blake, Emily Dickinson and the Hymnographers* (New York: New York Library Press, 1966) 119.

3. England and Sparrow 126.

4. Charles R. Anderson, *Emily Dickinson: Stairway of Surprise* (New York: Holt, Rinehart and Winston, 1960), 24.

5. England and Sparrow 119.

6. Johnson, *Biography,* 86.

7. David Porter, *The Modern Idiom* (Cambridge: Harvard University Press, 1981) 99.

8. Barton Levi St. Armand, *Emily Dickinson and Her Culture: The Soul's Society* (Cambridge: Cambridge University Press, 1986) 155.

9. England and Sparrow 129.

10. Porter, *Idiom*, 99.

11. Joseph Jones, *Poems and Hymn—Tunes as Songs: Metrical Partners* (New York: Norton, 1984) 3.

12. England and Sparrow 132.

13. David Porter, *The Art of Emily Dickinson's Poetry* (Cambridge: Harvard University Press, 1966) 143.

14. Johnson, *Biography*, 94.

15. St. Armand 337.

16. Albert Gelpi, *Emily Dickinson: The Mind of the Poet* (New York: Norton, 1971) 149.

17. Richard B. Sewall, *The Life of Emily Dickinson* (New York: Farrar, Straus and Giroux, 1980) 714.

18. England and Sparrow 116

19. Porter, *Idiom*, 4, 105, 104.

20. St. Armand 159.

21. Jane Donahue Eberwein, *Dickinson: Strategies of Limitation* (Amherst: University of Massachusetts Press, 1985) 143.

22. Anderson 26.

23. Sewall 714.

24. Willis J. Buckingham, ed., *Emily Dickinson's Reception in the 1890s: A Documentary History* (Pittsburgh: University of Pittsburgh Press, 1989), entry #79. This description appeared in the *Amherst Record*, January 7, 1891, p. 2, as a reprinted article from *The Springfield Republican* in 1878, whose author plainly argues that the author of the "Saxe Holm" stories was Emily Dickinson rather than Helen Hunt Jackson, as was generally believed.

25. Jones 25.

26. Preface to *A Garland for Emily*, as quoted in Carlton Lowenberg, *Musicians Wrestle Everywhere: Emily Dickinson and Music* (Berkeley: Fallen Leaf Press, 1992), 104.

27. James Davidson, "Emily Dickinson and Isaac Watts," *Boston Public Library Quarterly* 6 (1954): 142.

28. John A. Gould, letter to the author, February 19, 1997.

29. Noel Tipton, letter to the author, February 20, 1997.

Chapter V. Musical Meters in Dickinson's "Hymns"

1. For additional information on meter in poetry and music, see Alex Preminger and T.V.F. Brogan, eds. *The New Princeton Encyclopedia of Poetry and Poetics* (New York: Princeton University Press, 1993).

2. Jane Donahue Eberwein, *Dickinson: Strategies of Limitation* (Amherst: University of Massachusetts Press, 1985) 244.

3. Richard B. Sewall, *The Life of Emily Dickinson* (New York: Farrar, Straus and Giroux, 1980) p. 622. Here Sewall quotes from a letter Dickinson wrote to Joseph Lyman about the mid–1860s.

4. Dorothy Huff Oberhaus, *Emily Dickinson's Fascicles: Method and Meaning* (University Park: The Pennsylvania University Press, 1995) 160.

5. Willis J. Buckingham, ed., *Emily Dickinson's Reception in the 1890s: A Documentary History* (Pittsburgh: University of Pittsburgh Press, 1989) #418.

6. Buckingham #418.

7. Sewall 26.

8. Buckingham #145.

Chapter VI. Musical Settings of Dickinson's Poetry

1. Carlton Lowenberg, *Musician's Wrestle Everywhere: Emily Dickinson and Music* (Berkeley: Fallen Leaf Press, 1992).

2. Jo Ann Margaret Sims, "Capturing the Essence of the Poet: A Study and Performance of Selected Musical Settings for Solo Voice and Piano of the Poetry of Emily Dickinson," diss., University of Illinois at Urbana-Champaigne, 1986.

3. Donald N. Ferguson, *Music as Metaphor: The Elements of Expression* (Minneapolis: University of Minnesota Press, 1960) 71.

4. Richard B. Sewall, *The Life of Emily Dickinson* (New York: Farrar, Straus and Giroux, 1980) 40.

5. Sims 44.

6. Robert Starer, letter to the author, February 26, 1997.

7. Sara Hopkins, rev. of "Songs of Charles Ives and Ernst Bacon," *Emily Dickinson International Society Bulletin* 7:1 (1995): 7.

8. Evelyn Davis Culbertson, *He Heard America Singing: Arthur Farwell, Composer and Crusading Music Educator* (Metuchen, NJ: Scarecrow Press, 1992).

9. Brice Farwell, letter to the author, February 23, 1997.

10. Sara Farwell, letter to the author, March 25, 1997.

11. Marshall Bialosky, "Vocal and Choral Music Reviews," *Notes* 45 (1989): 861–863.

12. Page Swift, "Ernst Bacon: The Man and His Songs," D.M.A. diss., Indiana University, 1982, 55.

13. David Bradley, rev. of Songs of Charles Ives and Ernst Bacon, *Journal of Singing: The Official Journal of the National Association of Teachers of Singing* Nov.–Dec. 1995: 14.

14. William Fleming, "Emily Dickinson Returned to Life," *Syracuse Post – Standard* 29 April 1966: 7.

15. Hopkins, 7.
16. Kenneth Haxton, letter to the author, February 12, 1997.
17. Robert Starer, letter to the author, February 8, 1997.
18. Tom Rasely, letter to the author, February 16, 1997.
19. Stanworth Beckler, letter to the author, May 7, 1997.
20. Material on Otto Luening provided to me by his widow, Catherine Luening in 1997 and 2002.
21. Robert Train Adams, letter to the author, March 3, 1997.
22. Alice Parker, letter to the author, April 14, 1997.
23. Roy B. Hinkle, letter to the author, February 26, 1997.
24. Richard Hoyt, letter to the author, February 15, 1997.
25. Gerald Ginsburg, letter to the author, February 15, 1997.
26. Ronald C. Perera, letter to the author, February 16, 1997.
27. David Irving, letter to the author, March 2, 1997.
28. Emma Lou Diemer, letter to the author, February 5, 1997.
29. Lee Hoiby, letter to the author, February 7, 1997.
30. Carol Herman, letter to the author, February 7, 1997.
31. Paul Gibson, letter to the author, March 25, 1997.
32. Jules Langert, letter to the author, February 26, 1997.
33. Kenneth Haxton, letter to the author, February 12, 1997.
34. James Waters, letter to the author, February 11, 1997.
35. Sharon Davis, letter to the author, March 10, 1997.
36. Jay Rizzetto, letter to the author, February 27, 1997.
37. Dan Locklair, letter to the author, February 15, 1997.
38. Robert Baksa, letter to the author, February 3, 1997.
39. Due to the limitations of this discourse, the works of many other important composers have, of necessity, been omitted. Though the following list is only partial, I refer the reader to the musical settings of Aaron Copland, Leo Smit, John Duke, Vincent Persichetti, William Roy, William Jordan, Lori Laitman, Jake Heggie, Peter Child, and Max Morath.

Chapter VII. Musical Reflections on Dickinson's Poems and Letters

1. Willis J. Buckingham, ed., *Emily Dickinson's Reception in the 1890s: A Documentary History* (Pittsburgh: University of Pittsburgh Press, 1989) entry #480.
2. Letter to the author, February 26, 1997
3. Francis Otto Matthiessen, *American Renaissance: Art and Expression in the Age of Emerson and Whitman* (New York and London: Oxford University Press, 1941) 140.

4. Rita Aiello and John A. Sloboda, eds., *Musical Perceptions* (New York: Oxford University Press, 1994) 42.

5. Millicent Todd Bingham, *Ancestor's Brocades: The Literary Debut of Emily Dickinson* (New York: Harper, 1945) 13.

6. Buckingham, Appendix A, 552.

Bibliography

Abrams, M. H. *The Mirror and the Lamp: Romantic Theory and the Critical Tradition.* New York: Norton, 1958.

Aiello, Rita and John A. Sloboda, eds. *Musical Perceptions.* New York: Oxford UP, 1994.

Anderson, Charles R. *Emily Dickinson: Stairway of Surprise.* New York: Holt, Rinehart and Winston, 1960.

Bertini, Henri. *Bertini's Piano Method Complete: A Progressive and Complete Method for the Piano-Forte.* Boston: Oliver Ditson, n.d.

Bialosky, Marshall. "Vocal and Choral Music Reviews." *Notes* 45 (1989): 861–863.

Bingham, Millicent Todd. *Ancestor's Brocades: The Literary Debut of Emily Dickinson.* New York: Harper, 1945.

_____. *Emily Dickinson's Home: The Early Years As Revealed In Family Correspondence and Reminiscences.* New York: Dover, 1967.

Blackmur, R. P. "Emily Dickinson's Notation." *Emily Dickinson: A Collection of Critical Essays.* Ed. Richard Sewall. Englewood Cliffs, N.J.: Prentice-Hall, 1963. 78–87.

Bondesen, Poul. *North American Bird Songs : A World of Music.* Klampenborg: Scandinavian Science P, 1977.

Bradley, David. Rev. of *Songs of Charles Ives & Ernst Bacon. Journal of Singing: The Official Journal of the National Association of Teachers of Singing* Nov.–Dec. (1995).

Buckingham, Willis J., ed. *Emily Dickinson's Reception in the 1890s: A Documentary History.* Pittsburgh: U of Pittsburgh P, 1989.

Carlyle, Thomas. *On Heroes, Hero-Worship, and the Heroic in History.* The

Norman and Charlotte Strouse Edition of the Writings of Thomas Carlyle. Berkeley: U of California P, 1993.

Cody, John. *After Great Pain: The Inner Life of Emily Dickinson.* Cambridge: Belknap of Harvard UP, 1971.

Culbertson, Evelyn Davis. *He Heard America Singing: Arthur Farwell, Composer and Crusading Music Educator.* Metuchen, N.J.: Scarecrow P, 1992.

Davidson, James. "Emily Dickinson and Isaac Watts." *Boston Public Library Quarterly* 6 (1954): 141–149.

D'Olivet, Antoine Fabre. *Music Explained as Science and Art.* Rochester, VT: Inner Traditions, 1987.

Eberwein, Jane Donahue. *Dickinson: Strategies of Limitation.* Amherst: U of Mass. P, 1985.

England, Martha Winburn, and John Sparrow. *Hymns Unbidden: Donne, Herbert, Blake, Emily Dickinson and the Hymnographers.* New York: New York Library P, 1966.

Ferguson, Donald N. *Music as Metaphor: The Elements of Expression.* Minneapolis: U of Minnesota P, 1960.

Fleming, William. "Emily Dickinson 'Returned to Life.'" *Syracuse Post-Standard* 29 Apr.1966: 7.

Gelpi, Albert J. *Emily Dickinson: The Mind of the Poet.* New York: Norton, 1971.

Gould, John A. "Dickinsinging and the Art Thereof." Andover / Phillips Academy Magazine, 1989.

Hollander, John. *The Untuning of the Sky: Ideas of Music in English Poetry 1500—1700.* New York: W. W. Norton, 1970.

Hopkins, Sara. Rev. of "Songs of Charles Ives and Ernst Bacon." *Emily Dickinson International Society Bulletin* 7.1 (1995): 7.

Johnson, Thomas H., ed. *The Complete Poems of Emily Dickinson.* Cambridge: Belknap P of Harvard UP, 1979.

Johnson, Thomas H. *Emily Dickinson: An Interpretive Biography.* Cambridge: Belknap P of Harvard UP, 1955.

Johnson, Thomas H., ed. *The Letters of Emily Dickinson.* Cambridge: Belknap P of Harvard UP, 1986.

Jones, Joseph. *Poems and Hymn—Tunes as Songs: Metrical Partners.* New York: Norton, 1984.

Keller, Karl. *The Only Kangaroo Among the Beauty: Emily Dickinson and America.* Baltimore: Johns Hopkins UP, 1980.

Leich, Roland. "Setting Emily Dickinson's Poetry to Music: Notes for a Talk at the College Club." Pittsburgh, Pa: Privately Printed, ed. 1990.

Lenhart, Charmenz S. *Musical Influence on American Poetry.* Athens: U of Georgia P, 1956.

Leyda, Jay. *The Years and Hours of Emily Dickinson.* 2 vols. New Haven: Yale UP, 1960.

Lowenberg, Carlton. *Musicians Wrestle Everywhere: Emily Dickinson and Music.* Berkeley: Fallen Leaf P, 1992.

Lubbers, Klaus. *Emily Dickinson: The Critical Revolution.* Ann Arbor: U of Michigan P, 1968.

Matthiessen, Francis Otto. *American Renaissance: Art and Expression in the Age of Emerson and Whitman.* New York and London: Oxford UP, 1941.

Meyer, Leonard. *Emotion and Meaning in Music.* Chicago: U of Chicago P, 1956.

Oberhaus, Dorothy Huff. *Emily Dickinson's Fascicles: Method and Meaning.* University Park: The Pennsylvania UP, 1995.

Porter, David T. *The Art of Emily Dickinson's Early Poetry.* Cambridge: Harvard UP, 1966.

_____. *Dickinson: The Modern Idiom.* Cambridge: Harvard UP, 1981.

Preminger, Alex and T.V.F. Brogan, eds. *The New Princeton Encyclopedia of Poetry and Poetics.* New York: Princeton UP, 1993.

Rich, Adrienne. "Vesuvius at Home: The Power of Emily Dickinson." *Shakespeare's Sisters: Feminist Essays on Women Poets.* Ed. Sandra M. Gilbert and Susan Gubar. Bloomington: Indiana UP, 1979, 99–121.

St. Armand, Barton Levi. *Emily Dickinson and Her Culture: The Soul's Society.* Cambridge: Cambridge UP, 1986.

Sewall, Richard B. *The Life of Emily Dickinson.* New York: Farrar, Straus and Giroux, 1980.

Sherwood, William Robert. *Circumference and Circumstance: Stages in the Mind and Art of Emily Dickinson.* New York: Columbia UP, 1968.

Sims, Jo Ann Margaret. "Capturing the Essence of the Poet: A Study and Performance of Selected Musical Settings for Solo Voice and Piano of the Poetry of Emily Dickinson." Diss. U of Illinois at Urbana-Champaigne, 1986.

Small, Judy Jo. *Positive as Sound: Emily Dickinson's Rhyme.* Athens: U of Georgia P, 1990.

Stephenson, William E. "Emily Dickinson and Watts's Songs for Children." *English Language Notes* 3.4 (1966): 278–281.

Swift, Page. "Ernst Bacon: The Man and His Songs." D.M.A. Dissertation, Indiana U, 1982.

Thorpe, William Homan. *Bird-Song: The Biology of Vocal Communication and Expression in Birds.* Cambridge, Eng.: Cambridge UP, 1961.

Tipton, Noel. "Hymns and Emily Dickinson: The Power of Melody." *Chorus!* Vol. 4.2 (1992): 4–8.

Todd, Mabel Loomis, and Millicent Todd Bingham, eds. *Bolts of Melody.* New York: Harper P, 1945.

Weisbuch, Robert. *Emily Dickinson's Poetry.* Chicago: U of Chicago P, 1975.

Whicher, George Frisbie. *This Was a Poet: A Critical Biography of Emily Dickinson.* Ann Arbor: U of Michigan P, 1957.

Winn, James Anderson. *Unsuspected Eloquence: A History of the Relations Between Poetry and Music.* New Haven: Yale UP, 1981.

Wolosky, Shira. "Rhetoric or Not: Hymnal Tropes in Emily Dickinson and Isaac Watts." *New England Quarterly* 61.2 (1988): 214–232.

Index of Poems Cited

The Johnson number of the poem is given in parentheses. An asterisk indicates that the poem is quoted in full; other page numbers indicate where the poem is quoted in part or mentioned.

Index of Letters Cited

Index of Hymns Cited

General Index